AD Non Fiction

: cheating,
ious
ig

DISCARDED BY
MEAD PUBLIC LIBRARY

TIME HEELS
CHEATING, STEALING, SPANDEX AND THE MOST VILLAINOUS MOMENTS IN THE HISTORY OF PRO WRESTLING

JON CHATTMAN AND RICH TARANTINO
FOREWORD BY TOMMY DREAMER

First published by Pitch Publishing, 2014
Pitch Publishing
A2 Yeoman Gate
Yeoman Way
Durrington
BN13 3QZ
www.pitchpublishing.co.uk

© Jon Chattman and Rich Tarantino, 2014

All rights reserved. No part of this book may be reproduced, sold or utilised in any form or transmitted in any form or by any means, electronic or mechanical, including photocopying, recording or by any information storage and retrieval system, without prior permission in writing from the Publisher.

A CIP catalogue record is available for this book from the British Library.

ISBN 978 1 90962 630 0

Typesetting and origination by Pitch Publishing
Printed in Gutenberg Ltd

Contents

Foreword	9
1. Introduction – The Bad Guys Win	13
2. Top H.E.E.L.S	17
3. Touching A Nerve – The Fans Speak Out	36
4. As The Heel Turns – Make A List	95
5. Heel Of Fame – These Baddies Should Be Enshrined Somewhere	101
6. Drop-kicktionary	104
7. Heel Stables – The Good, The Bad And The Hornswoggle	108
8. Name That Tune – Heel Edition	122
9. Bad – We're Drawn That Way	127
10. Foreign Objects 101	143
11. How To Be A Heel – Twenty Badass Steps At Being A Badass	147
12. Movies Gone Bad	152
13. Heel Turns On The Fans	154
14. Dream Matches	160
15. What Heel Would You Want In Your Corner During a Zombie Apocalypse?	164
16. Heel Of The Moment – 100 Bad Guys Who Did A Whole Lot Of Good	166
17. Heels By Numbers	223
18. Heel Wrestlers A-Z – Last Will And Testament	228
Afterword By Jimmy Snuka	232
About The Authors	234
Special Thanks	237
Epilogue	243

For our tag team partners
Jaxon and Noah and the
future of wrestling fans
Alexander Miele

Sporting a Cubs hat at the St. Louis arch? Sporting a badass 'stache in general? Authors Jon Chattman and Rich Tarantino aren't afraid to unleash their inner heels.

Photographs by Peter Lederberg except Eddie Guerrero (Tim Harshman), Raven (Andrea Kellaway) and Snake (Andrea Kellaway).

Foreword

THE first time I saw professional wrestling I was hooked: 30 April 1979. On that date, the All-American WWE Champion Bob Backlund defeated Bulldog Brower who at the time I thought was the most dangerous man. He was a crazed killer wanting to destroy the goody two shoes Bob and take the coveted title. Bob took all this maniac had to offer and good prevailed over evil.

I was entranced with how these larger than life men could fight and bounce back: modern-day comic book heroes doing what they do…fight evil. I loved all the good guys and booed the bad guys. Yes, I was the perfect fan.

Then something changed. I watched Larry Zbyszko turn on his mentor Bruno Sammartino and break a wooden chair over Bruno's head, leaving his mentor face down in a pool of his own blood. I became enraged with the fact that a good guy would do this.

Why would he turn his back on his mentor? I remember actually crying. The difference between how I would watch wrestling before and just cheer someone because they were a good guy was why I became emotionally vested into my fan favourites. I wanted to tune in next week and see why Larry would do this. I couldn't wait to see Bruno return and get his revenge on Larry. I made my dad take me to Shea Stadium to see Bruno's revenge inside a steel cage. Even though my favourite wrestler Bob Backlund was on the card, I needed to be there for Bruno.

That emotional attachment has made me a wrestling fan since I was eight years old. I have seen some amazing wrestling angles when good guys have turned bad – whether it be for greed, a manager being in the ear of his new protege, someone not wanting to be in the shadows of their mentor or friend…whatever their skewed reason. I hated them.

Before there was the internet you would receive all your wrestling news through wrestling magazines. They had a ratings system as well as who was most popular and who was most hated. I couldn't believe when I saw Tommy Rich's face with the caption 'the fans can go to hell'. How could this good ol' boy do this?

I needed as much information as I could get. I have seen Barry Windham turn on his partner Lex Luger and join the Four Horsemen, Andre the Giant rip a cross off of Hulk Hogan's neck and turn on his friend. I have seen Shawn Michaels throw Marty Jannetty through a glass window and Randy Savage break up the Mega Powers with Hulk Hogan because he thought Hogan had lust in his eyes for Miss Elizabeth.

These memories and so many more are etched in this wrestling mind of mine.

I had an amazing wrestling career, always playing the defender of the good of ECW. I was turned on by many of my so-called friends. One of my favourite parts of performing is when fans would literally help me up when I was down and they were ready to fight evil with me. I became that larger-than-life superhero to them.

I hope you enjoy this book and you see how amazing it is when someone becomes emotionally invested in someone else…even when they're the bad guys. Thanks for reading.

Tommy Dreamer
May 2013

1
Introduction – The Bad Guys Win

FEW of us wanted the witch to get the best of Snow White. We highly doubt anyone wanted the Sea Hag to snatch away Sweetpea. You probably didn't root for Clubber Lang to beat that 'fool' Rocky Balboa, nor do you have a poster of Manuel Noriega on your wall. Yes, for the most part, no one really likes to see the bad guy win.

Well that is unless it's in the world of professional wrestling where the villains arguably out-rank, out-number, and out-perform the good guys. From the days of The Great Kabuki to the nights of the New World Order (nWo), wrestling baddies – or 'heels' in industry lingo but you know that already – have resonated with fans even more than the good guys. If you listen closely after reading that sentence, you'll hear John Cena getting booed somewhere.

Time Heels celebrates the notion that bad guys in wrestling do it better, and always have. For decades, or at least as long as Zach Gowen has been alive, wrestling has been called a soap opera for men and it's true…it's damn true.

Like the best soaps, some fans are torn between loving to hate the baddie (Alexis Carrington was one glorious bitch) and loving the good guys (Blake Carrington was lame). This constant see-saw of emotion is what has made this soap opera a hit with all the toothless wonders that watched wrestling in back alleys and in the territories to World Wrestling Entertainment (WWE) viewers of today. We would give the slight edge toward the villains, because they are the reason everyone keeps watching.

To make a crappy analogy, let's look at things this way: the pro wrestling platform is like a hot girl who doesn't know she's hot dating a jock who is the biggest douche in the world. As the story always goes, all of this girl's friends tell her she is with the wrong guy, but she stays with him even though there is a guy who would do anything for her – equipped with nothing but a good personality and good intentions.

Just as women are gravitated to the 'wrong guys', men are drawn to bad boys as well. Heels provide audiences with a sense of danger, and an element of surprise. Heels usually have the better mic skills, finishers, and managers in the business. There is a reason for that: they draw. Good guys? Well, they die young – just ask Billy Joel.

Introduction – The Bad Guys Win

If you look into wrestling history or ask anybody who was a fan before Vince McMahon Pac-Man'd World Championship Wrestling (WCW), people's disdain for heels drove a company or a territory. Manny Fernandez and Nikita Koloff put asses in seats because people wondered what they would say next to rile up the crowd. One of the reasons Ric Flair has had such a long career is because fans always wanted to not just hear what he would say, but they would be curious as to what cheap shot he would take out next on his opponent.

In the late 1990s, when the aforementioned and groundbreaking stable the nWo was reigning supreme, during each 'Hey Yo' promo Scott Hall did, he would take 'a little survey' to see if the audience favoured the good guys – in this case WCW – or his band of misfits. While the outcome wasn't as contested as fatties choosing between Samoas or Tagalongs, it always seemed that no matter what city the artist formerly known as Razor Ramon name-dropped, audiences went wild for the 'bad guys'. Ironically, Hall would always say, 'survey says… one more for the good guys'. It was the bad guys, however, who were too good not to root for.

We can drive this sentiment home, but we would rather start the book, which is a quirky look at the world of heels over the past 30 years or so. We count down the top heel moments of all time, ask grapplers to weigh in on their favourite bad guys of all time, provide wacky top ten lists of our favourite villainous trials and tribulations, and get a first-hand fan perspective of heel highlights that moved them.

Wrestling has its fair share of inspiring good guys, but the bad guys do it better – just ask those aforementioned sluts earlier who dated all those tools in high school. So let's get to it. Put on your tights, cue the entrance music, and get your ass into the ring. Hating wrestlers so passionately is what makes this great form of sports entertainment so damned likeable and addictive. They say time heals all wounds – well, we say heels have stood the test of time.

2
Top H.E.E.L.S

WRESTLING enthusiasts Jon Chattman and Rich Tarantino first began research for the H.E.E.L. Rating Scale as youths in the mid-1980s during separate trips to the Westchester County Center located in the suburbs of New York City.

As most pre-pubescent youngsters of this era were ogling at the sight of an animated Baroness in the G.I. Joe glory years, the brothers from different mothers were knee deep in LJN Superstars toys, foam fingers and *Piledriver* albums all while secretly in the early stages of creating this sophisticated formula for rating the most heinous acts in the history of professional wrestling.

What we aimed to do was not only rate the most celebrated moments of villainy in the squared circle but to take a closer examination at the impact these events had on the dastardly individuals that were closely involved while also focusing on the reaction of the fans, the entertainment value, the rise and fall of careers and the historic ramifications they had or continue to have in the ring both inside and out.

The scale was perfected over a period of 25 years through advanced research, countless hours of wrestling videos (which included the *Rock 'n' Wrestling* cartoon sans Mr Beefcake) and culminating with several trips to the capitol of pro wrestling, Parts Unknown.

As we all know, the key to being an effective villain in the world of pro wrestling is the uncanny ability for wrestlers to get fans to hate their guts. Whether it is through a charismatic promo, potent mic skills or an obvious disregard for rules followed by a blatant shot at a hapless opponent's man parts, the bad guy is essentially the most vital aspect of any wrestling angle and perhaps the best workers in the business. For several decades the heel has taken short cuts, rule breaking and foreign object use to new heights and thus the battle in the squared circle between good and evil has flourished.

These infamous antagonists have continued to run roughshod throughout the business and we felt that these larger than life performers, albeit a few bad seeds, should be showcased and remembered for their treacherous wrongdoings and over the top performances.

We have broken the H.E.E.L. Rating Scale into four separate categories with each being just as crucial as the next. Without any further ado here is the breakdown for each one:

Heat of the moment
Entertainment factor
Elevation of character
Longevity in the ring

We hope you enjoy this section just as much as we did researching it. It is not all here but there is a pretty good taste of flaming tables, higher power reveals, foreign objects, and Orndorff turns. Oh, and of course, the leg drop that broke our red and yellow hearts!

At-ten-hut!: The Sarge Joins Cobra... (Well sort of)

Heat of the moment:
Robert Remus has lived a truly great life in and out of the wrestling business. Best known by his guise as a United States Marine Corp. Drill Sergeant, Sgt. Slaughter has been 'cobra clutching' evil-doers for well over 30 years. With his popularity through the roof the American-made wrestler was even introduced into the G.I. Joe toy line as well as making appearances alongside Snake Eyes and Gung Ho in both the cartoon and comic book adaptation of the highly popular action figure franchise (take that Dwayne Johnson).

While some think his career in camouflage began in the ring, Remus was in fact a retired United

States Marine Sergeant turned pro wrestler. While he first started his rule-breaking ways against the Pat Pattersons and Bob Backlunds of the world, the future Hall of Famer soon turned face and began the defence of the American way in a bloody feud with the Iranian superstar, the Iron Sheik. Their historic feud culminated in an unforgettable boot camp match that headlined a sold-out Madison Square Garden crowd and helped turn Sgt. Slaughter into a household name among patriotic fans across the country.

While his path to the top never seemed to derail, much like the Lex Express experiment of 1993, Slaughter eventually made his presence known as part of the American Wrestling Alliance (AWA). After five years or so of wrestling in Verne Gagne's backyard the Sarge once again set his sights on WWE in 1990.

Slaughter, however, was not to return in his trademark stars and stripes this time around – he was aligning himself with the enemy. As tension between the United States and Iraq was increasing Vince McMahon decided to have the country's proudest son (that wasn't named Hulk Hogan) turn his back on Old Glory and support the cause of real life dictator Saddam Hussein.

Entertainment factor:
Albeit controversial the Slaughter turn was pure genius. Claiming America had gone soft the Iraqi sympathiser was soon donning Arab head-dresses along with his sheik-inspired curled toe boots. Adding

insult to injury the turncoat even began using the infamous camel clutch submission manoeuvre as his finisher. Although it made for some riveting television if truth be told, the venue for WrestleMania VII had to be changed to an indoor facility in light of death threats and security issues that surrounded the newly-found hatred the Slaughter gimmick ignited.

Elevation of character:
Feuding with Col. DeBeers across Minnesota can only get you so far so when Sgt. Slaughter captured the WWE Championship in January 1991 it was no surprise that he had fully reached the mountain top despite a controversial victory over the Ultimate Warrior. If winning the strap wasn't enough he reached top heel status the same year when he secured a match against the ultimate babyface Hulk Hogan on the grandest stage of them all.

Longevity in the ring:
You can bet Cobra Commander could not be any prouder of the treachery that Sgt. Slaughter dealt to Hogan and his band of wrestling heroes but despite being the top badass for the better part of a year the former champion soon took the Cpl. Kirchner route and was once again leading the 'U-S-A' chants in arenas across the country.

After a fully-fledged heel run Slaughter eventually became an on-air authority figure via the Jack Tunney route and he was soon the butt of D-Generation X jokes throughout the early years of the Attitude Era, even becoming one of McMahon's stooges for a short time.

Current-day Sarge, years removed from his greatest Benedict Arnold impression, still makes the yearly trip to WWE Raw where he is often jobbing to up and coming talent.

King Kong Bundy Crushes Little Beaver 29 March 1987

Heat of the moment:
More than 93,000 fans packed into the record-breaking Pontiac Silverdome on a legendary spring night that still remains as one of the most talked about events in the history of World Wrestling Entertainment. As Andre passed the torch, Piper was embarking on the first of his many retirements and Steamboat and Savage stole the show, it was a gimmick match for the ages that still resonates in the minds of devoted wrestling fans all over the world.

Standing at 6ft 4in and close to 500 pounds during his best heel run as a card-carrying member of the famed Heenan Family, King Kong Bundy stands as one of the most massive superstars of all time. The over-sized behemoth sent shockwaves throughout the industry during a mixed tag team match at WrestleMania III when he teamed up with Lord Littlebrook and Little Tokyo to face the threesome of Hillbilly Jim, The Haiti Kid and of course the 4ft 4in 60-pound Little Beaver who soon fell victim to the Walking Condominium's body slam and unforgettable elbow drop.

Entertainment factor:
Only in the pre-determined stage show of wrestling can we glorify the blatant disregard of the rules and just as brutal as it was to watch (and not brutal to watch in the Katie Vick storyline sort of way) it still trumps any and all elbow drops that have come and gone.

Elevation of character:
Sure, Bundy's brightest days were behind him as his headlining steel cage main event against Hulk Hogan less than a year before was clearly in the rear-view mirror.

However his claim as one of the industry's top heels was never in question despite him being relegated to a mid-card showdown with Hillbilly Jim and just two years removed from his nine-second squash of Special Delivery Jones at the inaugural showcase of the immortals.

We can only imagine that it was his public display of un-affection towards one of the more popular midget stars of his day that still kept him in the 'most hated villain' conversation.

Longevity in the ring:
Mainstream recognition was no stranger to Bundy but the sun soon settled on his main event career and he was soon gone from the WWE only to make a

brief return in the mid-1990s as a part of the Million Dollar Corporation. Remaining as one of the more recognisable combatants of his era, it is no surprise that in its heyday even his LJN figure can smash a solid window or two. These days a much slimmer version of the Bundy character can be seen cracking jokes on the comedy circuit, making the occasional indy appearance and most likely still posing a threat to little wrestlers the world over.

Memo to Hornswoggle – your 15 minutes should have been up years ago so maybe it is time for the New Jersey big man to re-introduce the avalanche to a whole new crop of *Raw* and *SmackDown* viewers.

Mega Powers Explode
3 February 1989

Heat of the moment:
Starting in 1987 and lasting for two years, wrestling universes collided when the worldwide phenomenon known as Hulkamania was able to co-exist with the Macho Madness of 'Macho Man' Randy Savage. Dubbed the Mega Powers, the superteam known best for its amped-up interview spots and over-the-top handshakes went in full motion during the climactic finish to WrestleMania IV's 14-man tournament where the immortal one, Hogan, helped his partner become the WWE Champion by smashing Ted DiBiase with a chair to set up a patented Savage elbow drop from the top.

The win not only catapulted the reign of the Macho Man but it also helped solidify the Mega Powers as the strongest force in the wrestling business. Although they never captured team gold their unity helped usher in the inaugural SummerSlam with a victory over the Mega Bucks (DiBiase and Andre the Giant) and an appearance by scantily-clad Mega Powers eye-candy Miss Elizabeth.

Of course in the wild world of pro wrestling nothing lasts forever, except of course Mark Henry's unexplainable push and Undertaker winning streaks. With that said the Mega Honeymoon was soon over. During a nationally-televised *Saturday Night's Main Event* during the winter of 1989 the company's two greatest faces of their era were embroiled in an epic showdown between the Big Bossman and Akeem the African Dream. Who knew that it would be the former One Man Gang who would start the rift between the two icons when he tossed Savage out of the ring and on to Elizabeth, knocking her out cold?

Hogan, being the goody two shoes that he was, carried the fallen goddess from the ring to the training area for some much needed 'medical attention'. When she finally awoke a disgruntled Hulkster returned to ringside but it was too late as Savage took his Twin Towers beating and was clearly pissed at the moustachioed Mega Power for abandoning him on prime-time television.

Despite being Macho-slapped by a distraught Savage, Hogan got the win for his team but as he arrived in the back to check on Elizabeth he was attacked by the champion who claimed Hogan was stealing his woman and his spotlight, sealing the deal for their eventual showdown at the fifth instalment of the Super Bowl of wrestling.

Entertainment factor:
The WrestleMania V match for the WWE Championship ran the suspenseful course we have known to grow and love over the golden wrestling years. A fully-fledged Hogan comeback followed by a big boot and leg drop ushering in yet another reign backed by the sea of red and yellow.

Savage, who was now in full heel mode, ditched the innocent valet gimmick and replaced the Mega Powers' manager with Sensational Sherri Martel, giving him instant bad guy cred.

The Madness also aligned himself with Tiny Lister, the actor turned wrestler known best as Zeus, leading to one of the more lesser known PPV events this side of This Tuesday In Texas, No Holds Barred: The Match, The Movie.

Elevation of character:
Despite coming up short against his Mega Powers partner, Randy Savage was still one of the industry's top superstars, which was capped by his coronation as the 'Macho King' after defeating perennial good guy Hacksaw Jim Duggan and using his royal sceptre to end the Ultimate Warrior's title run.

Longevity in the ring:
Randy Savage always made for a better heel and was making history as the guy fans loved to hate long before 'Stone Cold' Steve Austin and The Rock began headlining the Attitude Era. An eventual Mega Powers reunion came in the now-defunct WCW but the Monster Maniacs just never sounded right in the first place even though they captured our hearts once again by conquering Kevin Sullivan's Alliance to end Hulkamania. Soon enough it was like deja vu all over again as the Mega Powers traded spray cans and heel turns throughout the hostile takeover of World Championship Wrestling and not even the fake Sting was safe.

Et Tutu, Hulk Hogan?

Heat of the moment:
His 'Hollywood' persona and New World Order heel turn may get all the press, but for us, Hulk Hogan's first memorable bad guy role came in 1993 when he turned his back on the fans that made Hulkamania run wild by appearing as a wrestler-turned-nanny in the would-be comedy *Mr Nanny*.

It would have been bad enough for the Hulkster to have *Suburban Commando* in his arsenal but he opted to make this comedy, which tried to replicate the 'big guy playing against type' success *Kindergarten Cop* had three years prior. It played like a turd floating in the sandbox instead.

Entertainment Factor:
None – that is, unless you count watching the Hulkster dance around in a tutu and make breakfast for a pair of bratty white kids.

Elevation of character:
Appearing in a comedic flop with Sherman Helmsley didn't boost Hogan's run in WWE at all. But, it didn't deter fans from loving him any less and tuning in to watch him in the ring. Hulkamania continued to run wild for a few more years in WWE and WCW in spite of the tutu turn.

Longevity in the ring:
Hogan has made more stinkers than a 12-year-old boy after a Taco Bell meal. There has been *Thunder in Paradise*, *Gremlins 2*, and that unnecessary sequel to the 3 Ninjas franchise with Loni Anderson. Thankfully for the Hulkster, portraying super nanny Sean Armstrong and other lame film characters hasn't derailed his career. Not even a sex tape can stop the unstoppable Hulk Hogan. That said, there's a reason no 'Nanny 4 Life' t-shirts were ever made.

Ref Ref Whine

Heat of the moment:
Die-hard wrestling fans probably knew that WWE referee Danny Davis (real name Dan Marsh) wrestled under a mask for years as Mr X, but it came as a sur-

prise to most viewers when he retired his Foot Locker uniform in favour of Sweeney Todd-like wrestling tights.

The build-up of Davis as a heel was a natural progression. At the tail end of 1986, he was ruining matches for the industry's top babyfaces by calling quick pins and provoking disqualifications. Gorilla Monsoon, who with Bobby 'The Brain' Heenan made up one-half of quite easily the best announcement team the business ever had, had also questioned his character, noting how he probably took bribes from the heels he helped out.

Davis had a series of misfires as ref that led to him being stripped of his ref shirt and competing as a wrestler. Some notable matches included prematurely awarding Paul Orndorff a win over Hulk Hogan in a steel cage match (that call would be overturned), and a pivotal match between the Hart Foundation and the British Bulldogs during a 26 January 1987 edition of *Superstars* in which Bret Hart and Jim Neidhart double-teamed their way to a Tag Team Championship on Davis's watch.

As a result, fake WWE president Jack Tunney suspended Davis, and Jimmy Hart got him to join the Hart Foundation. Thus, 'Dangerous' Danny Davis was born.

Entertainment Factor:
Having Jimmy Hart in his corner just made us love to hate him even more. Danny Davis's re-branding to 'Dangerous' Danny Davis was a new storyline that we had never really seen before. We had seen babyfaces

turn bad, and managers betray their own 'clients' but we had never seen someone stop being a ref so they could fight guys in the ring.

It may not have worked had it been another personality (sorry Joey Marella), but Davis played the role of ref-turned-heel to a tee. And he wasn't a one-hit wonder. He helped secure wins for the Foundation by interfering in their matches, and won a six-man tag match with them at WrestleMania III.

Other highlights during his two-year run as a grappler included defeating Tito Santana and Junkyard Dog in the 1987 King of the Ring tournament, competing at the very first Survivor Series, and trying to steal Damien from Jake 'The Snake' Roberts. Seriously, who steals a snake?

Elevation of character:
Davis went from being a sub-plot to a main storyline in the world of wrestling, and his association with the Harts made him an almost instant top heel for over a year and, at the very least, a solid mid-carder. He also gave a mean Boston crab.

Longevity in the ring:
After a two-year-plus run, Davis's appeal went the way of the buffalo, and he eventually dusted off that Foot Locker uniform and became a referee again. By the early 1990s, however, he was off WWE television and a new era of crappy refs was born courtesy of the Hebner twins.

Train, Say Your Prayers, And Take A Clothesline

Heat of the moment:
It is fitting that 'Mr Wonderful' Paul Orndorff made his WWE debut on the same night Hulk Hogan beat the Iron Sheik to claim the WWE Championship at Madison Square Garden on 23 January 1984. The two grappling greats seemed to be associated with one another throughout most of the early 1980s – originally as foes, then friends, then foes again, and then, yes, friends again. One heel turn, however, stands out in the course of both careers.

It was 1986. The New York Mets were on a World Series run. America was runnin' on Fred the Baker and his Dunkin' Donuts. Eddie Murphy dappled in the music industry. That infamous year was also the time in which Mr Wonderful turned his back on his tag-team partner Hulk Hogan, and started a feud that ran longer than a *Dynasty* spin-off.

It all unfolded in the year following the very first WrestleMania. The Hulkster and Mr Wonderful were at opposite sides of the ring in that contest with Hogan partnering Mr T (with Jimmy Snuka in their corner) against the wonderful one and 'Rowdy' Roddy Piper (with 'Cowboy' Bob Orton in their corner).

In that epic main event, Hogan pinned Orndorff after Orton mistakenly hit him with the cast on his arm. The fall-out from the match included Orndorff firing his manager Bobby 'The Brain' Heenan on television, and engaging in feuds with his former partners Orton and Piper.

Orndorff's babyface about-face led him to run wild with Hulkamania. The two were an unstoppable force, but the wheels eventually fell off the bus. During their match against Big John Studd and King Kong Bundy, Orndorff let Hogan take a beating at the hands of the two large-and-in-charge superstars, and just when you thought he would help the Hulkster out, he turned faster than a *Walking Dead* zombie.

After he helped Hogan to his feet and raised his hand in the air, Mr Wonderful gave him – apologies to JBL – a clothesline 'from hell' followed by a piledriver. Thus, another feud was born, brother!

Entertainment factor:
Even a blind man could see this inevitable parting of ways, but the build-up to this eventual break-up between Hogan and Orndorff was extremely enjoyable. Whether it was Adrian Adonis getting under Mr Wonderful's skin by referring to him as 'Hulk Jr' or the 'accidental' bumps Hogan and Orndorff took from each other during their ring exploits leading up to the feud, this was wrestling storytelling at its best.

Elevation of character:
Paul Orndorff was arguably the biggest heel in the WWE during his 're-feud' with Hogan. Watching him re-unite with the Heenan Family really propelled him to great heights, and made him a bankable bad

guy for the company. More importantly, he became a man fans loved to hate. The Hogan/Orndorff steel cage match from *Saturday Night's Main Event*, which Orndorff lost, is still discussed today as was a match they had in Toronto that took place outdoors in front of – according to Wikipedia – about 76,000 fans.

Longevity in the ring:
Orndorff is a WWE Hall of Famer, and rightfully so, but the aforementioned feud with Hogan was the biggest push he would ever see – in the WWE anyway. Following another run as a babyface, he reteamed with the Hulkster at the first Survivor Series (with Don Muraco, Ken Patera, and Bam Bam Bigelow) and took on Oliver Humperdink to manage him, but a serious injury he sustained during the Hogan feud caught up with him and forced him to retire.

We all remember reading reports of his death in the late 1980s, but he actually retired and became the owner of a bowling alley (which in some circles may be worse than death).

Orndorff returned to wrestling shape in the 1990s, and wrestled on-and-off with WCW and the independent circuit with mixed results. He won tag team gold with a then known as 'Stunning' Steve Austin, and held his own in singles competition until injuries once again forced him to re-retire. He spent the rest of the 1990s training talent at the WCW Power Plant in Atlanta, and in 2005, Heenan inducted him into the WWE Hall of Fame – fittingly.

Marty Jannetty Is Not My BFF

Heat of the moment:
Toiling in the tag team division for years and competing against teams such as Demolition, the Hart Foundation and the Brain Busters, the Rockers were the pretty boy faces similar to the high-flying style of the Rock n' Roll Express. Shawn Michaels and Marty Janetty captivated crowds throughout the American Wrestling Alliance (AWA) until finally arriving in WWE all while hanging with some of the world's top teams. Eventually however the sun set on the charismatic duo and its impact continues to be felt to this day.

During a memorable visit to Brutus Beefcake's Barber Shop an emotional Rockers reunion seemed to be eminent after some recent close calls that were obviously setting the two apart. After appearing to settle their differences Michaels hit Jannetty with his now trademark super-kick finisher known as sweet chin music. Adding fuel to the fire, the mullet-haired melee was capped off by an enraged Michaels tossing his former friend head first through the window of Brutus's Barber Shop.

Entertainment factor:
This was one of the more memorable heel turns. Jannetty getting thrown through a window certainly upped the ante and made for a more entertaining finish to the end of the Rockers' run. It would turn out to be a downward spiral of sorts for the one-time

Intercontinental Champion who would eventually become the Andrew Ridgeley of the wrestling world.

Elevation of character:
While Jannetty embarked on mid-card mediocrity for the rest of his career his former partner has become one of the most recognised characters in wrestling history. The Heartbreak Kid has become synonymous with being a main event star and headlining some of the more classic WrestleMania matches in recent memory.

Longevity in the ring:
Since the shocking window shattering the two grapplers have gone in completely opposite directions. While one has made a Hall of Fame career and won every title known to man (even the WWE European Championship) and to this day continues to milk the 'Mania moment cash cow, his former Rocker mate is touring the independent circuit with Sean Waltman (known as the 1-2-3 Kid, X-Pac and various other names).

3
Touching A Nerve – The Fans Speak Out

ASK any wrestler – except perhaps the Ultimate Warrior (kidding) – and they'll tell you the fans make the business what it is. They help fuel the wrestlers' passions, and inspire them to raise their game to new levels. With that said, our next section takes you on a squared circle journey of first-hand accounts by the most loyal fan base you'll find in sports entertainment or sports for that matter. Read on…

When I first interviewed for my job at a direct marketing company, I was blown away when Joey Styles was the guy interviewing me, who ultimately turned out to be my boss. Upon finding out I was a wrestling fan myself, Joey would call former (and current) wrestlers he kept in touch with so that I could say hi. One day he told me he needed to go to the WWE building during lunch and asked if I wanted to join him. The whole ride down, he was talking about all the wrestlers we would see and how he would introduce me to them. Upon clearing security on our arrival, we saw Jim Ross walking through the lobby. Joey couldn't wait to introduce us and yelled his name. JR walked over and as Joey was asking how he was and how was the family, JR looked at him and said, 'Who are you?'

Rebecca A.
Harrison, New York

So it's day two or three of filming at Florida's Supercon; a giant geek fest full of bad smells, cute girls, and a whole lot of things I can't afford and want. Gotta love it. I'd been filming pro wrestling on and off since 2005 and I've learned a thing or two about the wrestling business, a key one being expect and accept anything. So when the following happened, all I could do was roll with it.

I'm just killing some time in between shooting, lolly gagging around when out of the corner of my right eye I spot a guy who looks suspiciously like Brian Knobbs of the Nasty Boys fame. Now being around wrestling for a while, I know this is the kinda guy I should seek advice from about trying to get a break in the wrestling business, even if the position doesn't fall between the ring ropes. He's been places, made money, and he's buddies with one of the biggest names, if not the biggest in wrestling. This is the kind of wrestler you can learn a thing from. So with nothing but humility in my heart, I approached Mr Knobbs.

Now Mr Knobbs was, as I quickly deduced, up to some form of shenanigans or another involving not paying parking. Smart guy like that. And as far as I knew, he was legitimately crashing a party he wasn't invited to, which from what I hear is typical Nasty Boys behaviour. Still, I wasn't going to let him get away without giving some advice so while I helped him in this little act of cheapskatery, I asked, 'Any advice for getting into wrestling on the production end?'

Mr Knobbs couldn't have been any nicer as he started to answer and was nothing but cordial in his response, and I've met wrestlers who were bigger 'stars' with way worse attitudes, so this was a wonderful interaction coming from someone who had zero reason to offer me anything, even the time of day. However what occurred next still can't escape my memory as being one of the strangest things I've ever dealt with in wrestling.

Without shame or hesitation, and while still carrying on the conversation as if it's no big deal, Mr Knobbs proceeds to pull down his pants enough to pull out his penis and piss on a tree outside the building, all while not drifting from the conversation in the slightest. All I could think was, yeah, this is wrestling.

He finished waxing philosophical on my question, 'be around and be seen', gathered his belongs, and went about his merry way. I will forever recall my first time meeting Brian Knobbs.

John S.
Pittsburgh, PA

Andre the Giant was the best WWE villain of all time in my opinion. He seemed unstoppable. He was the only wrestler that I hoped to beat Hulk Hogan back in the late 80s. He was literally a larger than life character and the only 'bad guy' I rooted for.

Joe Beninati

I have been watching wrestling as long as I can remember. Never forget the days watching with my grandfather and he would throw punches as if he was in the ring. I believe I finally got completely hooked during the Savage/Steamboat feud. In fact the greatest heel moment had to be the ring bell by Macho Man on to Steamboat's larynx. I know most would say Barber Shop window, or Hogan turn (most stunning), but Savage's attack was something for the ages and the pinnacle of heelage (that a word?). However my favourite heel was probably 'Ravishing' Rick Rude. No heel had the charisma that he had. Wearing tights with Jake 'The Snake' Roberts's wife on them is just classic. Making out with a woman from the crowd?! I mean brilliant. If I had to pick a top moment that I witnessed live I remember I was at a wrestling event at Westchester County Center. 'Cowboy' Bob Orton just defeated someone (can't remember who, but was a crowd favourite) by hitting them with his cast. When he was walking back down the aisle, some kid (about 13) threw a beer on to Bob. He reached over to try and grab the kid but to no avail. Security came flying over and went chasing after him. He showed that night what a great heel he was that he could get the crowd that fired up.

Franco S.

The WWE cartoon show *Hulk Hogan's Rock 'n' Wrestling* from the 1980s is what got me hooked into wrestling, as a matter of fact the evil Mr Fuji character was what roped me into watching the show. I think the fact that my grandmother had me watching old Charlie Chan shows is really what got me hooked on Fuji. Like most five-year-olds I gravitated to the good guy team of Hogan and the gang, but I always enjoyed Fuji and Piper on the cartoon show. The greatest heel moment in wrestling other than Mr Perfect sinking a backwards foul shot in one attempt would have to be Shawn Michaels turning on Marty Jannetty on the Barber Shop interview segment on *WWE Superstars* in the early 1990s. I say this because Jannetty's career never recovered from that super-kick through the window. Michaels went on to become one of the greatest wrestling superstars of his generation while Jannetty became a forgotten IC champ then fell even lower as a WCW jobber who opened up *Nitro* shows against Glacier and Das Wunder Kid Alex Wright. Also this was a major shock to me because the Rockers were the most popular tag team at the time. Best heels are in no particular order: Shane Douglas (ECW), Ric Flair, The Rock (with the Nation of Domination and The Corporation), Hall and Nash, Raven, 'Rowdy' Roddy Piper, Randy Savage, Scott Steiner, Curt Hennig,

Rick Rude, Steve Carino, The Dudley Boyz (ALL OF THEM including Joel Gertner), Bobby Heenan, the Million Dollar Man.

Greasy Griswald

As a kid I was drawn to the WWE Intercontinental Championship for a number of reasons: the mental exercise of trying to figure out the domain that an 'Intercontinental Champion' reigned over (Eurasia? A vast swathe of the Atlantic Ocean? Perhaps the Bering Strait?), the perceived dynamism of the title as it changed hands on a frequent basis (at least compared to the Hogan-dominated WWE Championship), but most of all the lowered expectations the title held. Who needs all the adulation of being the best in the world? Set your sights a little lower and even you, Greg Valentine, can strut around with a sweet belt knowing that you're the toughest man on the Intercontinent.

The heel in my story is actually one of the most prolific babyfaces of the WWE's 'What about a wrestling dentist?' era: Bret 'The Hitman' Hart. Let me explain. My favourite wrestler in those days was Mr Perfect, AKA Curt Hennig; my allegiance being won the day I found out we shared a first name. It doesn't take much when you're nine years old.

My available memories of wrestling snap into focus in the third grade, around the time when Mr Perfect clowned some dude from Texas whose finisher was a spin punch (or something) for the IC title. The next nine months of Saturday mornings were filled with lucky charms and video packages of my favourite wrestler throwing 100-yard touchdown passes to himself, bowling perfect games, and running pool tables in empty rec rooms. Life was pretty good.

I wished I could see his excellent finisher, the Perfect Plex, more often but he didn't actually wrestle that much. When he did, his matches typically ended with ace manager Bobby 'The Brain' Heenan incurring a disqualification (which, along with 'double count-out', is one of the most reviled terms among nine-year-old wrestling fans). I realise now that this qualified Mr Perfect as a heel, but at the time I thought, 'If he could just get on a good roll he wouldn't need all of this outside interference to keep the belt.'

I figured his SummerSlam 1990 match against the Hitman would be the perfect showcase for his under-appreciated talents, especially with the meddlesome Heenan out of the picture and some nitwit with a clipboard in a filthy sweat suit in his place at ringside. The new guy didn't look like he could tie his own shoes, let alone influence the outcome of a serious professional sporting event. Plus Hart's claim to fame to that point was as a tag team wrestler, and everyone knew those guys didn't go anywhere once they went solo (see: Dream, Akeem the African).

I hunkered in with my snack food spread out on the floor in front of me and my eyes wide. Halfway through the match, Perfect dropped one shoulder strap from his singlet: the sign that he was officially done screwing around. When he executed his patented front roll snap-

mare, I put a two-litre bottle of Pepsi on ice. When he nailed Bret Hart with the Perfect Plex (catnip to my nine-year-old brain) I reached to pop the cork, eyes dutifully trained on the 17-inch tube TV in my bedroom.

Then the unthinkable happened: Hart kicked out. I instantly tried to rationalise: maybe Perfect didn't hook it in 100 per cent? Was that a slow count by referee Earl Hebner? As the seconds passed and Hennig unsuccessfully lobbied the official, I felt my brain try to adapt to this new landscape. Nobody ever kicked out of the Perfect Plex! It would have been less of a shock to my system if my parents walked into my room and began speaking to me in Russian.

As you have probably guessed, Mr Perfect lost the belt after four and a half more minutes of stunned silence and a failed intervention by the homeless man who had been skulking ringside. What you might not have known was that Mr Perfect effectively didn't wrestle for a year and a half after SummerSlam due to a real-life back injury he sustained some months earlier. So not only was I subjected to some tag team wrestler in hot pink tights and blu-blockers holding my favourite title belt, but Mr Perfect all but disappeared from the scene without even an inquiry from the office of WWE president Jack Tunney.

To add insult to injury my parents started buying Wheat Chex instead of Lucky Charms, which congealed to the consistency of moist sawdust before I could even get the bowl to the living room. Saturday mornings sucked in a big way.

I guess you could say the real heel was the bulging disc in Mr Perfect's back, but that won't stop me from looking back with vitriol toward Bret Hart for ending the splendour of Hennig's reign. The Panama Canal and the Aleutian Islands will never raise a finer champion.

Kurt R.

On the 5 November 2007 edition of *WWE Raw* from the Staples Center in Los Angeles, I was looking to do some research for my MA thesis on professional wrestling. I had not been to a live WWE event in a couple of years, and I was really looking forward to this event.

One thing that I noticed was that more families were in attendance than when I had last attended. In observing the audience before the show started, I could not help but overhear a young couple in their 20s with a three- or four-year-old child. It seemed like this was the child's first WWE event. Instead of being excited for the show, he was petrified by one WWE Superstar – The Boogeyman.

For nearly a half-hour before *Raw* went on the air, the parents assured their scared son that The Boogeyman would not appear because he was only on *SmackDown*. This was pretty much the gospel truth because the brand split was enforced pretty well in WWE at the time. *SmackDown* stars typically stayed on *SmackDown* while *Raw* stars usually stayed on *Raw*.

Raw started with its typical fanfare of fireworks and music of course. Shawn Michaels and Triple H were in the throes of one of their many 'One Night Only' DX reunions. Everyone wanted to join DX it seems. Firstly, Hornswoggle wanted to join, but he was informed that he was not on the list so he put Michaels in a short-arm scissors proving his worth to DX. This provided some comedy to start off *Raw*.

The DX comedy continued as Triple H asked Hornswoggle to check under the ring. Hornswoggle would not check there claiming a monster was hiding beneath the ring. The warning bells went off for the family behind me mildly, and I heard the wife behind me say, 'Oh no,' quietly. Her husband reassured her and their son that The Boogeyman was only on *SmackDown* and could not be on *Raw*.

In the ring, Michaels went to check what was going on under it. He was pulled under and quickly returned but with a surprise in his mouth – earthworms.

Less than a minute later the lights started to flash in the arena and red smoke filled the ring. The Boogeyman's eerie music started to play with its signature 'I'm coming to get you' voiceover.

Loud cries from a young child rang out behind me with shouts of 'Oh no,' 'This was not supposed to happen here,' and more cries. This child was beyond consoling as he bawled, whined, cried, shrieked, kicked and hit trying to get away. Every nightmare of The Boogeyman came to life right in the Staples Center live on *Monday Night Raw*.

Even though his parents tried to rush him quickly out of their seats and into the comfort of the hallways with fast food and merchandise, they were not fast enough.

Suffice to say their night ended far too early not because of The Boogeyman but because of not realising that nothing is for sure in the world of professional wrestling.

This little boy could yell, could scream, and could cry his eyes out all he wanted. His parents made a promise to him that they should not have made, and I wonder what they say about all of this today. I hope they can have a laugh about it.

In all his epic red and yellow make-up, furs, and twisted wooden staff sifting smoke, The Boogeyman assured one little boy and his parents on this 5 November 2007 evening that anything could happen in WWE and gave a twisted memory to me.

Sean McCallon
@TheBlueMask246
sean.mccallon@gmail.com
Seanmccallon.com

Most people will tell you that Hulk Hogan turning on all his vitamin-popping Hulkamaniacs was the greatest heel turn. But lest we forget most apple pie eatin' Americans had seen him take on Rocky Balboa as Thunderlips and knew he had it in him. The real twist to the gut of the Red, White, and Blue was when Sgt. Slaughter went from cobra clutch to Cobra. The former G.I. Joe action figure had apparently been upset that Nikolai Volkoff had his own heel turn on Mother

Russia and felt fans had gone soft. Why was this heel turn so great? It led to a title and WrestleMania headline match as most successful heel turns usually do. Which brings me to my next point; how great was Kim Chee? The true extent of the fortitude and complexity that was Kim Chee can only be magnified by the digression made by the rigorous non-diet of Kamala.

As for Skandor Akbar...he's no Admiral Ackbar. If I had to choose a winner of a heel battle royal I would go with Road Dogg who had quite possibly the greatest Royal Rumble strategy of all time. Grab the bottom rope and hold on. While the gravitational pull takes its toll on the heavyweights the right-hand man of Mr Ass had the master plan.

When it comes to foreign objects no one compares to the black armband of Iron Mike Sharpe. Has there ever been a more nefarious non-factor in the history of grappling? Clearly, the pedlar the Sharpe family bought this from hosed them by selling them the least lethal metal armband known to man. If there was any psychological factor in the ring it was hardly noticeable, however it seemed to be good enough to make him a greater Canadian athlete than Wayne Gretzky, Joey Votto, and Steve Nash.

Al Yankovich
Straight Outta' Stamford, CT

The greatest heel in wrestling is Terry Funk. I remember when I was about seven or eight watching WWE shows and Terry Funk would come out with his branding iron and brand everybody he would beat after the matches and leave the double cross ranch branded on them all. What a crazy guy and such a bad guy. He also used a chainsaw as Chainsaw Charlie and the greatest was against Ric Flair. Funk was a judge or something for Flair's match against Ricky 'The Dragon' Steamboat and after the match he went to shake his hand and instead of shaking his hand he beat him down and gave him a piledriver on top of a table. This was before any ECW stuff and before they were using tables all the time. To me he was definitely the top of all the bad guys. In ECW he would fight in all the hardcore matches and in Japan he was crazy, he had all those barbwire and bomb matches with Cactus Jack.

First of all if I had to pick a winner for an all heel battle royal I would make it a Royal Rumble match. I think my winner would either be Ric Flair or Edge. Ric Flair was one of the greatest if not the greatest of all time. He proved that he could win a Royal Rumble before so I think he has the best shot. I would put him, Kurt Angle and Roddy Piper as the last three. Flair would out-smart the both of them but it would be a classic match-up. They should just give them microphones, I would probably watch that also.

Edge is one of the top bad guys in recent years. He has proved himself to be a bad guy after he stole Matt Hardy's girlfriend and he cashed in his briefcase twice to win the world title.

My favourite foreign object of all time is the megaphone that Jimmy Hart, 'the Mouth of the South', would use to help his tag teams win every match. I also liked the Hulk Hogan helmet he used against Bad News Brown. It had a fist on it.

The greatest heel moment, I would say two of them. Well one is not really a heel moment but when Undertaker tossed Mankind off of the cage on to the announcer's table. The other was when Nexus beat up John Cena and trashed the set of *Monday Night Raw*. Another one and also a great heel moment was when Raven made Sandman's son turn on Sandman back in ECW.

Steven Harrison

Looking back over the years I spent working for wrestling magazines, refereeing matches, or working in the front offices of promotions it's hard for me to pick just one incident. To me, the best heels have a true, real aura of danger combined with a sense of unpredictability that makes them such great wrestlers to hate.

There was the time that Terry Funk got pissed that I took a picture of him yelling at ringside fans and he chased me and another photographer around the ring waving his branding iron. Another memorable time was when The Original Sheik threw a fireball behind my back. I turned around after hearing a loud 'whooooooosh' to see all orange and had to drop on to my back to avoid the fire. Or there was the time when Abdullah the Butcher was fighting in the back parking lot of a plaza and he threw his opponent through the back door of a dive bar thus scaring all of the drunken patrons as they fought on the pool tables.

Oh, and the pain was all too real at times. Whether it was during a referee gig that 'Ragin' Bull' Manny Fernandez drilled me in the mouth for trying to physically break up his brawl with Jules Strongbow or the Iron Sheik chopping the hell out of me at ringside and leaving his whole hand print in my chest.

And those are just the ones that spring to mind but I love my memories of the heels.

Timothy Harshman

We The Heels

'In professional wrestling, a "heel" is a villain character. That is to say, heels are the supposed "bad guys" in professional wrestling storylines. They are typically opposed by a face (crowd favourite).

'Some "tweeners" (not explicitly regarded as good or bad) exhibit heel mannerisms.

'Heels are often portrayed as behaving in an immoral manner, breaking rules or otherwise taking advantage of their opponents outside the bounds of the rules of the match.

'Others do not (or rarely) break rules, but exhibit unlikeable personality traits. No matter the type of heel, the most important job is that of the antagonist role.

'Heels exist to provide a foil to the face wrestlers. If a given heel is cheered over the face, a promoter may opt to turn that heel to face, or to make the wrestler do something even more despicable to encourage heel heat.'

Source: Wikipedia

We the heels do not need permission to execute our plans. We decide who, we decide when and there is no guarantee we will either show up to a match or stay until the end.

It is our prerogative to demand championship opportunities and we cost others theirs in favour of our own.

The truth is, we can do whatever we want. We are not constrained by rules and regulations. Sympathy and morality are for the weak-willed. There are rules in the world of heels of course but never forget that winning is everything!

Did you honestly think we were your friend or ally? You are only in the spotlight because we say so. Your sole purpose is to serve the greater good: our own.

Heels are arrogant, self-serving, self-involved, cocky, bold, conniving, calculating and treacherous.

We will strive to annihilate all competition to ensure victory through careful planning and sometimes, even destruction. There can be only one…better us than them.

We can also be made to appear weak in the face of danger. Often we run away when the odds look impossible but never forget that the objective is to win therefore we will live on to fight another day when the conditions will suit our agenda, not yours.

We the heels are not always without heart. We have valets and tag team partners. Managers promote us because they know we are exciting and filled with potential.

We have better in-ring gear too, cooler entrances and since we do not need the approval of the fans, it is so easy and liberating to just be ourselves.

Like cats chasing mice, we also love to play with our food. Why not just get it over with and pin your opponent one may think, the obvious answer is: because we are having so much fun.

We the heels are impressive and send shivers down your spine.

There are countless examples of magnificent villainous characters throughout film and literature: Melkor, Sauron, Darth Sidious, Darth Vader, Magneto, Apocalypse, Mr Sinister, Sylar, Miranda Priestly, Sephiroth, Lord Voldemort…the list goes on and on.

In wrestling, heels also marked history and became some of the greatest characters to ever grace the squared circle.

Names like Ric Flair, The Undertaker, and Triple H and in recent years, Randy Orton and CM Punk, all picked up the ball where the good guys failed.

They have held countless championships, became favourites despite their evil ways and portrayed some of the most interesting personas the world has ever seen.

It ain't easy being a heel…wait actually, it is.

We the heels will neither apologise nor beg for forgiveness. We may fake it from time to time but we do not need anyone's pity.

'Lie, cheat, steal' were the words of Eddie Guerrero, one of the best villains to walk this Earth.

Those words are golden since they reflect what we, the heels are all about: winning. Does that bother anyone? Does it make anyone get angry?

By now, everyone should have gotten the point that we heels do it to get a rise out of you.

In the list opposite, that fabulous one that describes what a heel is, a few more words were forgotten.

We the heels are also scandalous and provocative. Like Depeche Mode sang years ago, no one can get enough of Melina's splits, Mickie James's psychotic, stalking behaviour, Kharma's laugh and Beth Phoenix's raw power.

Lita has live sex celebrations with her boyfriend, Edge. Stephanie McMahon dumped Test for Triple H…duh!

The Divas of this business know how to be feisty and manipulative. Behind a great man stands a great woman, often enough. Chicks with attitude…we the heels like that a lot. What can be cooler than that?

As much as people say they hate her, everyone really loves Vickie Guerrero. 'Excuse me!!' must be the most heat-drawing line ever created in professional wrestling. It's as if a nail is driven deep inside everyone's head as soon as it leaves that woman's mouth. That is the point!

Can villains show respect? Of course we can. We are not robots.

A truce can always be beneficial in the long run. It must not however, be seen as any sort of act of kindness because if one person should be stupid enough to let their guard down then they are done for.

The snake will strike…and win again! Just ask Randy Orton and 'Stone Cold' Steve Austin, the deadliest predators in all of wrestlingdom.

There is another phrase that may soon drive people insane: we the heels. Someone somewhere is about to start thinking, 'If he says we the heels one more time…!'

There will be a rare occurrence on this day…a bad boy who will show mercy, just this once and hold back.

I am Giulio alias the Phoenix. I am a heel, a villain and loving it.

Giulio Romano
@JayPhoenix77

I've been watching wrestling every since I was born. My father was a HUGE wrestling fan (he went to the Shea Stadium matches with Bruno Sammartino v Stan Hansen and also Sammartino v Larry Zbyszko) so he got me into it at an early age.

My first wrestling moment that I could remember though was a few months after WrestleMania III, they showed the Butch Reed v Koko B. Ware match on 'free TV' and although I was already watching it, that's the earliest memory that's etched in my head.

Since that was a throwaway match more or less, the coolest 'first' memory that I have of wrestling was when Strike Force defeated the Hart Foundation for the tag titles in October of 1987. Back then title changes didn't happen as frequently as they do now, so when that happened it literally felt like the biggest moment of my life at the time.

A few of my favourite heel moments in pro wrestling were Roddy Piper breaking the coconut over Jimmy Snuka's head on Piper's Pit and hitting Captain Lou Albano with a 'platinum record' in the build-up to WrestleMania I. This helped cement Albano's face turn and got Piper even more over as a force to be reckoned with.

Ric Flair and the Andersons breaking Dusty Rhodes's ankle in a cage. Ric Flair (a face at the time) is getting attacked by the Koloffs after a match. Dusty Rhodes runs in to make the save and runs away the Russians. Flair pushes Rhodes and tells him that he didn't need his help. Ole and Arn Anderson run in from behind and attack Dusty and instead of helping him out, Flair locks the cage and joins in on the attack. This led to the formation of the Four Horsemen.

Randy Savage hitting Ricky Steamboat with the timekeeper's bell and 'crushing' his larynx was an AMAZING angle and of course led to one of the most amazing matches of all time. As you can tell, I'm partial to the 1980s. Some more recent heel moments that I've enjoyed were Evolution turning on Randy Orton right after Orton became the youngest World Heavyweight

Champion in WWE history. Randy Orton giving a DDT and then kissing an 'unconscious' Stephanie McMahon on her forehead while Triple H is handcuffed to the ropes unable to do a thing. When Orton kicked Vince McMahon in the head a few weeks before that was really good as well. Jericho throwing HBK through the 'Jeritron 3000' was awesome. That entire storyline was amazing and was the first time in his career that I could say that I truly 'enjoyed' Jericho's work.

Nexus attacking John Cena was probably the most 'out of nowhere' thing that the WWE has done (other than Punk's promo) since the Attitude Era. It legitimately felt so chaotic that even though you knew it was a part of the show, it still stood out more than most attacks typically do. I was watching the show with my girlfriend and she was literally so uncomfortable watching it that she had to turn and walk away. She's a big John Cena fan so watching him get beat up by eight guys was particularly hard for her to take. That clearly shows you that it struck a nerve with some of the audience which is the amazing thing about pro wrestling when it's done right.

My favourite heels in pro wrestling:

Ric Flair: As a kid I hated him so much since he would always talk so much crap, get his ass beat for the majority of the match and somehow walk away with the belt still in his hand. It wasn't until I got older when I became 'smart' to the business that I realised not only was Ric Flair doing his job, he was doing his job about as well as anyone had ever done before him or since.

CM Punk: He reminds me a lot of an 'old-school heel'. Nowadays too many of the antagonists are 'trying to be cool' and in doing so they come across more likeable than some of their counterparts. After he turned in the summer of 2012, Punk was legitimately disliked by more crowds than any heel I've seen in the last five years. Every time they tried to like him, he would ultimately say something that would make them despise him even more than they did before.

I think part of the reason why Punk is so successful is because he's such a student of the game (cliche alert). I had a LONGGGGG conversation with Punk about ten years ago about the history of wrestling (his favourite heels, favourite feuds etc.) and he was so passionate about what he thought was good and what he thought wasn't that it only makes sense for him to have as much pride in being a bad guy as he does.

I was able to sit down and have lunch with Shane Douglas (during WrestleMania weekend in Miami). Shane is a guy that I respected a lot in the 1990s (right as the internet and ECW were really hot) who I thought would become a bigger star in WWE than he was. He was telling me why he felt it didn't work out and why it was doomed from the start. He also said that guys like HBK, Hall and Nash were consistently lobbying to keep him down.

Regardless, he had an amazing career in ECW (him throwing down the NWA belt after winning it in a tournament was a moment that stands out particularly) and WCW (liked him better as a face as Ricky Steamboat's partner) and I think will be remembered fondly by a lot of fans.

I had Kevin Steen spit at me and my girlfriend at a Resistance Pro show (Billy Corgan's promotion) in Chicago about a year and a half ago.

It was one of the few wrestling shows that I've been to that had a full bar available so we took advantage of that as the night went on. It was held at a nightclub in downtown Chicago and there were only about 100 fans there so needless to say the crowd's words tended to travel. Steen was in the main event against Harry Smith and we decided to jump on him a bit. After a few minutes of heckling, Steen hocked a big loogie in the direction of us. Thankfully he didn't hit us spot on but we got the gist of it.

Nicholas Masci

As a child of the 1980s my favourite was the duo of I.R.S. and the Million Dollar Man. What could be worse than being super greedy about money? Think Alex P. Keaton on steroids. Really. [Also] Jim Lawler v Andy Kaufman. He was a total bad guy but turned out to be a good sport. Athletes can be funnier than comedians.

Krisana Soponpong

A friend and I met 'Rowdy' Roddy Piper at a convention in Indianapolis in the summer of 2012. Piper was especially talkative at his merch table, and asked my friend, 'What was the first wrestling match you watched?' My friend answered with Macho Man Randy Savage against Ric Flair at WrestleMania VIII. Upon reflection, I realised that my first real exposure to wrestling, I believe at age five, was a Papa Shango vignette, hyping his introduction to the World Wrestling Federation.

For those unaware (and I'd imagine if you picked up this book and are aware of who I'm talking about, you already have chills of embarrassment shooting up and down your spine), Papa Shango was a wrestling character of a voodoo priest, loosely based on a spirit of Haitian voodoo, Baron Samedi. It was portrayed by Charles Wright, who would later go on to much more reputable fame as the Godfather (a wrestling pimp; just because I said reputable fame, doesn't mean I meant morally reputable).

The character is, to this day, a groan-inspiring memory of probably every wrestling fan that lived through the post-steroid, cartoony era of wrestling (I mean specifically cartoony by comparison to pro wrestling in general, of course). For some reason, this guy intimidated me so much that I just had to keep watching.

My wrestling fandom took on a life of its own shortly thereafter. Although Hulk Hogan was obviously my favourite character, guys like Bret Hart, Sting, and Shawn Michaels kept me coming back for more (and more, and more, and...). It was my dream to one day grace the squared circle and test my might against the largest athletes in the world. Then, when

I was 13 years old, my dream came true: in a dirty backyard, within the confines of a ring comprised of filthy mattresses and presumably the only petrified wood Home Depot had to offer.

Under the moniker of C.M.F. (not sure what kind of content this book is allowed to have, so let's just say it stood for Crazy Manatee Fighter), I found my childhood dream to be nothing short of exhilarating. At a time when backyard wrestling promotions were all the rage of parents' nightmares, I was gifted with a 'promoter' (the quotes are not a shot at the guy at all; I just wasn't sure how to address his title within the context of the story) who actually taught us how to more or less wrestle without hurting each other too much, or at all.

Each Saturday afternoon, I got to live out my dream… of gingerly performing wrestling moves on other guys my age to the jeers and ridicule of my peers. It wasn't the most encouraging start, but it was still a start.

After about a year of my being in this promotion, I received the news that we were ditching the backyard, and moving to a legitimate wrestling building with a real ring and everything, which ended up being the famous Doghouse, in Jamaica, NY. Upon arriving, as a 14-year-old white kid from a less-than-frightening neighbourhood in Queens, New York, I was pretty terrified. Hanging around during our first show were pretty imposing looking dudes who were probably not from the same less-than-frightening neighbourhood that I was from. To top it off, I had the unenviable task of performing in my promotion's first match in the new building.

Wrestling with (or against, depending on how you look at it in hindsight) a close friend of mine, who had actually helped me get involved with the backyard promotion in the first place, we awkwardly tussled and fumbled our way around a very unforgiving (remember, we were used to mattresses) ring for what felt like six hours, with all the grace of a pair of three-toed sloths. I like to refer to this match nowadays as the Murphy's Law Death Match; everything went wrong, with or without our power.

After several similarly terrible exhibitions in our new, somehow more hostile surroundings, I decided to seek out help and actually learn how to wrestle, as opposed to the 'more or less' style that I had been honing for the year or so previous. A friend who was light years ahead of me in the art of wrestling worked diligently with me on every basic nuance of wrestling, and the results were quickly pretty clear (or at least by comparison to my previous work, anyway).

Although I fell out of the wrestling game with the closing of the Doghouse in 2002, I still can never explain the thrill of being (slammed and tossed about, for those smarmy readers) in a ring, and the fun that coincides with learning what you're doing every step of the way. However, if I were to attempt to explain it, I would say that the simulation of body language mixed with human emotion is nearly intoxicating.

Sure, it hurts a bit. But in the brief and fleeting time I got to live out my childhood dream, no matter how bad life seemed with school and relationship drama, everything seemed right with the world when I was in a ring. I have recently decided to give it another go (at the ripe old age of 26, of course).

And I have Papa Shango to blame for this desire/obsession. If you watch some of my earlier matches, you would probably see this as fitting.

Nicholas Silverstein

In 1989 I was living in Winston-Salem, NC…Tobacco Road. The heart of redneckery. I had become a big fan of Monster Trucks (go Grave Digger) but hadn't caught on to pro wrestling yet. At a sleepover, my friend 'Cleve' told me that he had a video, which would get me into wrestling for sure. That video was the recording of MTV's *The War to Settle the Score*. This came about as a result of Piper's kicking Cyndi Lauper in the head during his interview segment earlier in the year…Hulk Hogan got involved and the feud was born. Being only seven years old, I was pretty much convinced that wrestling was the realest and coolest thing in my little universe. Second only to Ninja Turtles maybe. I spent the rest of my time in Carolina being a solid wrestling fan and saw some great careers and feuds. I DID always wonder how Sting could beat up on guys twice his size though…I'm sure steroids had nothing to do with it. lol

Ryan Will

I'll never forget when I was younger my older sister's boyfriend at the time and my across-the-street neighbours took me to see a steel cage match between Sgt. Slaughter and the Ultimate Warrior (Sensational Sherri days). I remember my sister's boyfriend picked me up (I was like nine at the time) and as the Warrior entered with Sherri I reached out for a piece of the Warrior and happened to grab Sensational Chest ha-ha. She looked at me and smiled and all the older guys were dying with laughter. Ha-ha. Middle of the match the Nasty Boys came out and raised all hell…

Mike Notar

By far, the greatest heel moment in the last generation is Hulk Hogan turning at Bash at the Beach 1996 and joining the nWo. Hogan, throughout his years in the WWE, cemented himself by creating a larger-than-life character and Hulkamania. Despite this, he shocked the world by his actions on that night in Daytona Beach. As a result, it refreshed his character, and left an indelible mark in the annals of wrestling history.

Yesterday's heel was given to an entirely different breed of wrestling audience. There was a clear distinction between a 'good guy' and a 'bad guy' and promoters made sure to differentiate the two in order to protect their top names. Moreover, it protected the purpose of their top names.

For example, NWA/WCW's top name was Ric Flair, who was a heel. Although there were some cheers for him, he would still do dirty tactics to get jeered, as well as keep his alliance with the Four Horsemen. His role was protected, so he could put the next babyface over in line, and help propel their career as a main event star. Namely, Sting, Lex Luger, and Ricky Steamboat, among others.

Today, Ric Flair would get cheered for the character traits he had in the 1980s, because the face/heel divide has gotten quite murky. This is why we have people like CM Punk and Dolph Ziggler getting cheers, while those such as Sheamus and Kofi Kingston usually are not unanimously cheered. The 1980s Hogan – on the other hand – would not be that same larger-than-life character, because that is no longer the kind of babyface who is appealing to the current audience.

Similar to how he won the 1992 Royal Rumble, Ric Flair in my book would win an all-heel battle royal. We would see him in spurts, but he would let all the other wrestlers duke it out until the end, where he would run behind the last two participants and eliminate them as they are trying to eliminate each other.

If I were a heel wrestler, without question, brass knuckles would be my foreign object of choice. Throughout the years, heels using brass knuckles have been the ones who had the least chance of being caught, as they can slide them right back in their trunks. We have seen how the babyface is on a roll, momentum continuing to churn, only to cease when a heel knocks them out with some brass knuckles as they are attempting a backdrop.

Chris Featherstone

The future never happened...There is a reason Dusty Rhodes was never elected President of the United States of America in 2000, and it has nothing to do with his yellow polka dot wrestling trunks. The 'son of a plumber' would most likely have had an everyman mantra that would have been relatable to most members of the electorate, but his potential presidency was kyboshed by the time-travelling hijinks of the New Breed.

The New Breed, comprised of Chris Champion and Sean Royal, travelled via a 'space bridge' from 2002 to NWA circa 1987. About the only thing they got right while screwing up the space-time continuum was that the Beastie Boys '(You Gotta) Fight for Your Right (To Party!)' would still be popular in the early 21st century.

In between name-dropping Autobots and Decepticons, the New Breed segued from flux capacitors to deleting their nemesis Lazer Tron (whom they believed to be an actual robot) from time itself. The coiffure-challenged duo also took a disliking for the Boogey Woogey Man, whom they labelled prehistoric and warned of their future tactics.

While wrestlers like Ronnie Garvin were busy working out, Royal and Champion would regularly return to 2002 to be 'physically upgraded'. The New Breed often boasted that 'all we do is get inside the squared circle and do business 2002 style' or 'in 2002 we've been partying like its 1999 for three years now'.

And therein lies their fatal mistake, when travelling through time...don't talk about the future. Thus the potential Dusty Rhodes presidency was wiped from time (however they appear to have been marginally successful in deleting Lazer Tron).

The past decade would've been drastically different with an 'American Dream' POTUS…at the very least we would've been spared the presence of Goldust (how could any presidency survive that?!).

Although they preferred space cycles to mopeds, someone de-railed the careers of Royal and Champion with a career-ending car accident. Perhaps it was the Rock 'n' Roll Express, Midnight Express, or time paradox created 11:59 Express that sent the driver to run down the New Breed. One thing is sure, Sean Royal was trapped in the past with a job as a construction worker and the world never got to see Ms Sapphire as the First Lady.

Albert Yankovich

One of my favourite heel turns was when Paul Orndorff turned on Hulk Hogan and rejoined the Heenan Family. The Andre turn was gold but Orndorff piledriving Hogan was awesome. Another heel turn I remember well was when Manny Fernandez turned on Jimmy Valiant and joined the Paul Jones Army. I loved it when Fernandez hit Valiant with the Halliburton full of money. The Valiant–Jones Army feud was a very under-rated feud of its day. Who could forget when Ron Garvin took J.J. Dillon and Gary Hart's money to knock out Dusty Rhodes during Dream's match with Barry Windham for the US title during the Great

American Bash? The image of Garvin rubbing his chest with the money was priceless.

Glen Braget

When I was a kid, I hated when Rick Rude would come out. I didn't like his ego and the way he strutted down to the ring. Thinking back on it now, his character would be awesome today. He did have a spectacular moustache.

IAmDynamite drummer Chris Phillips

My childhood got super-kicked! Being a casual wrestling observer in my adulthood, I base my interest in a particular wrestler on what I feel are the obviously important aspects: in-ring ability, showmanship, mic skills, and general badass-ery.

As a die-hard wrestling fan in my youth, this was not so. As is the case with most children, I operated under the assumption that life was a clear-cut, black-and-white, endeavour (good or bad, face or heel, Pamela Anderson or Yasmine Bleeth). Easily swayed by the writing and marketing staff of WWE (because they're great at their jobs), I cheered for the 'good guys' like they just rescued my grandmother from a tree, and I booed the 'bad guys' like they just stole my cat's Social Security cheques.

In the years before I hit double digits, there were no wrestlers cooler to me than the Rockers, Shawn Michaels and Marty Jannetty. Their proficiency as a tag team was thrilling to watch. Their entrance music was rad. They had awesome hair (mullets were cool once, right?). Every facet of their characters drew me in, and it was blatantly obvious to me that these were the 'good guys'. They very well might be a subconscious reason I'm pursuing a career that revolves around rock stars.

Shawn Michaels was, without question, my favourite of the two. Everything about Marty Jannetty was pretty cool, but everything about Shawn Michaels seemed just a bit cooler. Although given my affinity for the wrestling abilities of Dolph Ziggler, I might just have a thing for blonds.

Following weeks of miscommunication and rising dissension in their ranks, the Rockers appeared on Brutus 'The Barber' Beefcake's interview segment, the Barber Shop. It seemed that my favourite tag team was patching things up. Then, after their heartfelt embrace, Shawn delivered sweet chin music to Marty, and then threw him through the glass window of the set. Not only was the kick perhaps the most technically proficient one I've ever seen Shawn deliver, but its impact was felt far beyond Jannetty's face.

The Heartbreak Kid's super-kick left me momentarily dumbstruck, then utterly…wait for it…heartbroken (see what I did there?). The Rockers were one of the earliest examples of best friendship that I saw, and here that friendship was disintegrating before my ten-year-old eyes, thanks to a betrayal I couldn't understand perpetrated by a man I had held in the highest regard not ten seconds earlier.

Ironically, or perhaps fittingly, it was Shawn Michaels who was the catalyst for my maturation out of wide-eyed childhood wrestling fandom and into a more discerning world of wrestling adolescence.

Before the Hardy Boyz, Edge and Christian, and the Dudley Boyz used it as a precarious platform upon which they built a legacy, the ladder match was synonymous with the name Shawn Michaels. The first ever ladder match was between HBK and Bret 'The Hitman' Hart. This match was featured on one of the two VHS tapes that I would rent every time I visited my Grammy (the other one was *Passenger 57*. Always bet on Wesley Snipes. Unless you're betting on who is not gonna go to jail for tax evasion).

At WrestleMania X, Shawn took on Razor Ramon for the Intercontinental Championship. It was the one that set the standard for years to come. The match had a tremendous amount of build-up. Following an extended absence, Shawn maintained that he was still the champ, a fact contested by Razor, who currently had the strap around his waist. It was decided that both belts would be hung from the legendary rafters of Madison Square Garden, and an undisputed IC champ would be crowned on the grandest stage of them all.

Following a splash delivered to his opponent from the top of the ladder, Shawn Michaels once again left me dumbstruck. It was my first 'Holy $#%!' moment that was simply about the athleticism and not the storyline. I was in awe not just of the athletic feat itself, but also of the gut reaction such a move inspired within me. I didn't care that Shawn was the bad guy. I didn't care that the competitor I was rooting for had just been squashed into the canvas. I just knew that I had witnessed something truly awesome.

Razor ultimately climbed the ladder and emerged victorious, and I felt great confusion. I cheered Razor's win, but I applauded Shawn's performance.

Shawn is the reason why, in subsequent years, I always pulled for Triple H, The Rock, and Steve Austin (when each was in their respective 'heel' phases). The Heartbreak Kid was also, for me, the Eye-Opening Kid. You know, because my eyes had been metaphorically closed, and Shawn metaphorically opened them.

Andrew Plotkin

A heel revolution… Remember the days when the good guys were revered and bad guys jeered? Remember the times when the heels were so vilified, they were booed out of each arena? Kiss those days goodbye: a revolution has arrived.

There has been a complete turnaround in the wrestling world. Wrestling fans now cheer heels. The wrestling world is trying to adjust to this phenomenon. It is not as black and white as it used to be, even though wrestling organisations try. Gone are the days of the Rock and Wrestling Connection, where Hulk Hogan defeated each bad guy he fought including Roddy Piper and the late 'Macho Man' Randy Savage.

WWE's goal is to get the fans rallying behind their heroes. John Cena is their 'Superman', never quitting and always doing the right thing. Kids buy into Cena, quite different from adult fans that mainly root for Cena's opponents. In those matches duelling chants can be heard. 'Let's go Cena!' from kids and the significantly louder 'Cena sucks!' from adults.

When did this happen? When can we really say the tide turned for the heel? Can we blame it on the arrival of the New World Order in World Championship Wrestling? The nWo consisted of Hulk Hogan, Kevin Nash and Scott Hall who were heels that transcended time because of turning Hogan, known forever as a wrestling hero, into a bad guy. It changed the face of the wrestling world like no one had ever seen before.

Hogan, Hall and Nash were the main heels since they formed at 1996's Bash at the Beach. They destroyed the entire locker room, defeating every wrestler they faced until something fascinating happened. Everyone in WCW started joining the nWo and eventually spun off into the fragmented Wolfpack and the Latino World Order.

The nWo's ranks got out of control, with fans eventually cheering for the New World Order. However at this point, heels were predominantly still being booed.

Many pondered, 'Could this have been the work of "Stone Cold" Steve Austin?' Before Austin became the face of the Attitude Era for WWE, he floundered in mediocrity in his heel persona. In 1996, Austin won the King of the Ring tournament against Jake 'The Snake' Roberts. Austin took the podium to speak to then-announcer Michael Hayes. The words Austin uttered next would change the face of professional wrestling, making him a bona fide star.

'You sit there and you thump your Bible, and you say your prayers, and it didn't get you anywhere! Talk about your psalms, talk about John 3:16… Austin 3:16 says I just whipped your ass!'

No one in WWE at the time had said 'ass' on live television. The next night, a revolution was born. Austin 3:16 signs flooded the arena on *Raw*. T-shirts were made saying 'Austin 3:16' and are still sold today. Is Stone Cold responsible for the heel revolution? No, many would argue he's not.

Austin went on to become a full-face, while he fought Triple H and Vince McMahon, two men who lived and breathed the heel role. They were incessantly booed out of arenas on every occasion. They represented the old-school heel: antagonising the crowd, using cowardly tactics and doing whatever it took to win matches. It didn't matter if they cheated or not to win; they didn't care about the fans. They knew their jobs and performed them to perfection.

So if Austin and the nWo are not responsible, who is? Blame it on national television.

It may sound far-fetched, but the small screen played a significant role in influencing fans. In 1999, HBO entered the scene with legitimate competition for the basic cable networks. They debuted a show called *The Sopranos*. David Chase created the drama about the Soprano family in New Jersey. James Gandolfini, who played mob boss Tony Soprano, head of organised crime in North Caldwell, New Jersey, committed heinous crimes. *The Sopranos* captivated audiences for seven seasons. Fans clamoured for more from Gandolfini, the ultimate 'heel', and the rest of the cast and crew. Its popularity resulted in other networks bringing their own 'anti-heroes' to the small screen.

If viewers hadn't connected to his portrayal of Tony Soprano, would they have even had the chance to connect to Michael C. Hall's portrayal of Dexter Morgan in *Dexter*? The same can be said for AMC's *Breaking Bad*, where a cancer victim turns drug dealer Walter White, or Vic Mackey the corrupt cop with a heart of gold in *The Shield*. These series spurred the development of more shows with anti-heroes. Television hasn't been the same since the birth of Tony Soprano.

From the wrestling perspective, who is the Tony Soprano of the wrestling world? Who became the heel that captivated audiences and turned the fans on his side? Enter Phillip Brooks, better known to the wrestling world as CM Punk.

Punk, whose contract was expiring in WWE in July 2011, would face John Cena at Money in the Bank in Chicago. On 27 June 2011, Punk helped R-Truth defeat Cena in a tables match. He then took a microphone and said some things that shook up the wrestling world.

Punk criticised the direction WWE went and how he was passed over because of wrestling politics. The frustrated Punk stated how he was the best wrestler in the ring, on the microphone and even at commentary, but yet still hasn't gotten the recognition he deserved. He insulted Vince McMahon and his family, The Rock and even Hulk Hogan. No one was safe from Punk's verbal onslaught. In fact, Punk acknowledged the existence of other wrestling companies including New Japan Pro Wrestling and Ring of Honor. They cut off his microphone midway through his promo, but it was too late. The 'pipe-bomb' went off, and the wrestling world was turned on its head.

Wrestlers reacted in favour of Punk's work. Legends like 'Stone Cold' Steve Austin and Shawn Michaels praised Punk's promo. Mick Foley stated the following on his Twitter account on the night of the promo, 'I have no idea where this @CMPunk thing might go, but I know I'll be watching. Captivating stuff.'

They weren't the only ones. Punk served a suspension as part of the storyline and missed the next Raw. Punk returned to Raw in Boston, Cena's home town, and arguably got more cheers than Cena, who was the face of their feud. This resulted in Punk's face turn and began his 434-day reign as WWE Champion. He turned heel before it ended, but the fans didn't boo Punk. They only cheered for him more, even when Punk tried to get the fans cheering against him.

Punk would only get heat from the crowd when squaring off against the Undertaker at WrestleMania 29. Even then, the crowd split with duelling chants for both men.

CM Punk is the Tony Soprano of wrestling heels. He took the crowd and captivated them into rooting for the bad guy. It is why Daniel Bryan's 'YES' chants worked. It is why Dolph Ziggler got cheers even though he's been a heel for the majority of his WWE career.

Fans root for the heels they love. In turn, they become good guys but not like Cena. They remain themselves in their character but don't evolve into Cena's personality. They're still the same heels we love. They just wrestle on the good side now.

The nWo became an army rebelling against WCW only to splinter into beloved groups. 'Stone Cold' Steve Austin led a one-man revolution until everyone else decided to follow him. CM Punk did the same as Austin and still leads that revolution, but he got what he wanted: recognition as a top name in the wrestling universe.

Fans root for the heels because they are captivated by their words and actions. These aren't the days of Ric Flair anymore. This era belongs to the heels, and we are in the midst of the HEEL revolution.

Sebastian Maldonado
@SebastianTSU

As a nine-year-old 'little warrior', very few things scared me more than Papa Shango. Sure in terms of actual wrestling skills he was little more than a jobber, but what was so frightening about Papa was the fact he didn't need to get his hands on his opponent to hurt him. In fact he didn't even need to be in the same room.

To this day, the image of my favourite wrestler, the Ultimate Warrior, violently upchucking with black ooze running down his face due to one of Papa's spells is still etched into my memory. I think when Kane debuted a couple of years later he might have taken the cake as the wrestler with the creepiest persona, but due to Papa's feud with the Warrior and my age at the time, Papa will go down in my mind as the creepiest wrestling villain of all time…even if he came back as the Godfather.

Rich Nardo

Late one Sunday afternoon in the mid-1990s I was playing in the woods with my best friend James Wrigglesworth. Our business there was the top-secret construction of a den made from branches and bracken. We had almost completed the wigwam style dwelling when James said he had to go in for his tea. He asked me if I'd care to join him and I said thanks, but no, I was going to stay and finish the den. Then James told me that earlier in the week his dad had installed Sky TV and tonight he was going to watch WWE.

Everybody at school was talking about it, but most had never seen it. For some reason, only people that lived on council estates and the very rich could afford Sky TV, and Sky TV was the only place you could watch WWE.

I saw the Undertaker for the first time that night. The arena went dark. Then suddenly a clap of thunder echoed out of the television and bounced around the living room. Flashing strobes cut through clouds of fog like lightning before an electric blue colour filled the screen and silhouetted his huge frame. He was wearing a long, black coat and a black fedora. An organ began to play and he walked slowly towards the ring. We were entranced.

I forget who the Undertaker fought that night, but he became my favourite based exclusively on the fact that he was the guy that won the first WWE bout I ever watched. There were others I could've chosen: the British Bulldog, who was born just down the road; Hulk Hogan, the popular choice; 'Macho Man' Randy Savage, because his name is fun to say. But, despite having no idea what his name meant, I went with the Undertaker.

I became obsessed with collecting the WWE collector cards in that determined way that only a ten-year-old boy can. Every Saturday I'd take my pocket money to the corner shop and buy as many cards as I could for one pound until I'd collected them all.

Then they released the action figures and I got the Undertaker for my birthday. Because I had no other WWE figurines I would match him up against Darth Vader, Mumm-Ra, and Skeletor in an intergalactic Royal Rumble of villains.

My love affair with the WWE was short-lived. Soon after that first encounter with the Undertaker I was off to high school where my attention turned to music and the unsuccessful pursuit of girls.

A few years later my mother sold my Undertaker figurine at a car boot sale for five pence. I watched as his new owner clutched him in his grubby little hand and walked away, taking a relic of my childhood with him.

Jon Langford
English musician and writer based in New York City. He is the bassist in The Chevin and has written for MLSsoccer.com, *Artrocker* magazine and ContactMusic.com.

Professional wrestling sunk its hooks into me and solidified my fandom in 1993. I had been viewing pro wrestling since the mid-1980s as a small child, but it was the feud between Jerry 'The King' Lawler and Bret 'The Hitman' Hart in WWE that reeled me in.

I was always a fan of the 'bad guys' in pro wrestling. These heels created magic in the squared circle through their ability to rile up audiences. Jerry Lawler is a master at the craft of being a heel, and his attack on Bret Hart at King of the Ring 1993 made a ten-year-old kid a fan for life.

Hart had earned the King of the Ring title, crown, and coronation by defeating three WWE Superstars in one night: Razor Ramon, Mr Perfect and Bam Bam Bigelow. This was no small feat as all three were established superstars in WWE. As Bret Hart was about to celebrate his rule over the WWE kingdom, a new villain sprung to attack who would claim to be the real king of pro wrestling.

This attack surprised me as a child, but I was excited to see the direction that this feud would take. Lawler soon became one of the top heels in WWE by talking tough when Bret Hart was not around but cowering in Hart's presence. I loved this feud because Lawler made it personal by attacking not only Bret Hart but also his family. Often joking about the age of Hart's parents, Stu and Helen, Lawler drew the ire of WWE audiences at the time with his brashness.

In a series of heelish promos and cheating tactics in the ring against jobbers, Lawler would demonstrate why he believed he was the only king in WWE. He further showed his heel-streak by feigning a leg injury from a car crash and claiming he could not wrestle Bret Hart at SummerSlam 1993. Having the evil Doink the Clown take his place in the match, Lawler soon attacked Hart with his crutch proving he was not injured at all. Such tactics made Lawler the type of heel that fans came to hate in WWE during 1993–1995.

The feud between Jerry Lawler and Bret Hart helped to set up Owen Hart's masterful heel turn that officially took place at Royal Rumble 1994. In a series of vignettes, Lawler revealed that Owen Hart was the 'black sheep' of the Hart family while Bret received all the accolades.

Lawler and Hart would continue to feud on and off into 1994 and 1995. Lawler might be a fun-loving commentator on *WWE Raw* today, but his start in WWE was as a hated heel.

Favourite heels:

Jerry 'The King' Lawler: His feud with Bret 'The Hitman' Hart during the early 1990s utilised classic heel tactics but brought an element of personal hatred that was rarely seen in WWE at the time.

Raven: During his ECW run, Raven utilised psychological heel tactics that bordered on the psychotic in 'brainwashing' The Sandman's son Tyler and his wife Lori Fullington.

His feud with Tommy Dreamer lasted for years in ECW and in the storyline had a connection to their childhood. These elements helped to make Raven's promos seem entirely real. Raven's unique style in dress connected pro wrestling to grunge fashion and music of the 1990s as well.

Taz: No one was tougher in ECW than Taz. With his hard-hitting style and devastating suplexes, Taz was a brutal killing machine without a soul. He helped to blur the line between sport and entertainment in pro wrestling. His loud and obnoxious manager, Bill Alfonso, helped to make him a great heel out of the ring with strong promos.

Mark Henry: 'The World's Strongest Man' is one of the best heels in WWE. He backs up his words with an incredible strength and toughness rivalled by none. Henry has shown that there is a place for the 'monster heel' in pro wrestling today.

Jeff Jarrett: 'Double J' Jeff Jarrett is my favourite persona in pro wrestling ever because of how utterly ridiculous he was. A WWE Superstar that claimed he was a Nashville country-singing superstar but could not get a record contract was novel at the time to me. His 1995 lip-synching performance of 'With My Baby Tonight' only caused people to dislike him more.

Sean McCallon
@TheBlueMask246
sean.mccallon@gmail.com
Seanmccallon.com

The heel turn is perhaps the most magical moment in all of professional wrestling. Nothing excites and confuses the crowd quite like one of their favourite faces suddenly losing it and changing sides. It creates more drama than anything else in that particular business. And drama is that for which the fans are there.

The best heel turns combine three key elements: surprise, betrayal of friends/stable mates, and betrayal of the fans. When these three elements come together in such a way, true magic is created. All three of my favourite heel turns exemplify this pristine moment.

My first favourite heel turn took place at an EEW independent wrestling show at Extreme Entertainment Wrestling's first ever Bash at Jones Beach. The main event pitted the champion Steve Sposili (myself) against former champions the Sweater Pimp and Big Daddy Dom in a triple threat, falls count anywhere match. At the time Big Daddy Dom and I were in the same stable. It seemed a no-brainer that the belt would stay in the 'family' if nothing else.

But just when everything seemed in hand, Big Daddy pulled the greatest heel turn in EEW history. Did he smash his stable mate? No. He laid down for the Sweater Pimp and allowed himself to be pinned. The referee, P. Daddy Justice, was also in the Dom-Sposili crew at the time, making it a double heel turn.

There was definitely surprise, as no one, not even the champ, saw it coming even while being jumped by preliminary wrestlers. He betrayed a friend and handed his belt over to a former enemy. And he betrayed the fans who loved me and couldn't stomach another title reign by the Sweater Pimp.

But it also had an additional element not present in any other heel turn, at least nowhere near to the same degree: it made absolutely no sense. Big Daddy Dom didn't even benefit from the flip. No belt, and another loss on his record.

The second heel turn I mention was on a much bigger stage than EEW's efforts. It was mid-1980s WWE at the Mid-Hudson Civic Center, in Poughkeepsie, NY. The main event saw Hulk Hogan and 'Mr Wonderful' Paul Orndorff square off with Big John Studd and King Kong Bundy.

Late in the match, the Hulkster was taking a beating at the hands of his opponents. Orndorff and the fans were screaming for the tag. Hogan was knocked back, smashing him into Mr Wonderful and knocking him from the ring apron. Bundy and Studd made the most of the opportunity and beat on Hogan even more. It only ended when Orndorff recovered and beat up/chased off the villains.

At that point he helped his hurting partner to his feet. He then raised Hulk's arm in a show of victory. Right as the cheers of the crowd reached its peak, Mr Wonderful did the unthinkable. He delivered one of the stiffest clotheslines I have ever seen to the Hulkster. No one saw it coming. He then beat on an injured Hogan, inviting Bundy and Studd back into the ring to join him in the beating.

I was eight when this happened. I was also live at the event when it happened. I believe that was even the event where I could be seen several rows from the ring when it was aired the following Saturday morning. I think that's why my betrayal felt so real. I was there when it happened.

No talk of heel turns could ever be complete without referencing the greatest one in professional wrestling history. When Hulk Hogan did the unbelievable and joined the nWo, turning his back on Randy 'Macho Man' Savage and Sting, no one had any idea. Hogan could never be the heel. He was THE face in and of professional wrestling. Never before or since has any wrestling fan been so betrayed by their opinions of their favourite wrestler than when Hogan and crew reminded everyone that in professional wrestling there is no such thing as certainty (except maybe the Undertaker winning at WrestleMania, but now I've probably jinxed that).

It led to WWE becoming second fiddle to WCW (and the nWo). It changed everything. Nothing was sacred in wrestling after that. And it led to the fiercest real-life competition between national wrestling promoters. And the fans won. That is why the heel turn is the most magical, dynamic, and dramatic event in all of professional wrestling.

Steve Sposili

'The Model' Rick Martel was always my favourite! He turned on Tito Santana when he realised that Tito was the weak link in Strike Force. Then he wisely hired Slick to guide his career. His genius career move came when he launched his own cologne, Arrogance. He would come to the ring spraying it so fans could sample this scent before it took the world by storm. He even gave Jake Roberts a sample once, to help cover up that BO. So Martel was definitely my favourite villain growing up, since he was cocky, arrogant, and one of the most underrated technical wrestlers ever in WWE.

Rob Hanson

WrestleMania X7…a competitive match between the two biggest WWE faces of the day, of all time really, Austin and The Rock. Neither was your traditional white-hat hero, so nobody was expecting a turn. At least I wasn't expecting one. This was a time in my life where I had tuned out of wrestling for a long stretch, but my interest had been rekindled by the Attitude Era, the Monday Night Wars, the rise of ECW, and all of those other awesome industry highs that have kept me watching regularly since. But for this particular show, I was only good for the occasional cable show (pre-DVR) and a pricey night of 'Mania on pay-per-view.

So maybe it was my fault that I didn't anticipate the turn. Wrestling can be so predictable; maybe I hadn't been watching regularly enough leading up to the show to see what was coming from a mile away. Or maybe, just maybe, this was one of those rare moments of shock and awe, of masterful ring work and brilliant psychology, where everything clicks and the usually predictable scripted sports entertainment is truly surprising.

Austin was growing frustrated over the course of the match, trying and failing to put The Rock down. Vicious as he was under normal circumstances, Austin's roughneck facade began to crack and then crumble, and desperation kicked in. The moment the turn was clear to me, the moment 'Stone Cold' Steve Austin shed his Texas Rattlesnake skin and revealed a true villain was when he broke out his old Ringmaster move, the Million Dollar Dream.

I thought to myself, 'Oh crap, he just went bad.' It was a new evolution and a brilliant call-back to what came before, all in the same choking manoeuvre. And that mark-out moment added legs to a rivalry and a company that needed a smart shake-up to keep that golden age shining bright. Man, I don't even remember who won the match, but I remember the moment The Ringmaster returned.

Matt Bergin

When I was a kid, wrestling from the Olympic Auditorium in Los Angeles was must-see TV for my brother and I. Dick Lane called the wrestling matches – he of 'whooooaaaaa Nellie'. I can't recall the good guys nearly as well as I can the bad. And no one, at least to me, was as bad a guy as The Destroyer. With his mask and his gravelly voice, he oozed mean. But there was also something alluring to him. Why did I like this masked guy? I know I wasn't alone.

ABC-TV NY anchor Bill Ritter

It's been a bit, but I remember it being pretty scary and bad ass when that dude Earthquake stepped on the bag containing Jake 'The Snake' Roberts's snake which was either Lucifer or Damien while Jake was tied to the ropes. I had a pet snake at the time.

Isle of Rhodes drummer Colin Behram

One of my favourite heel turns was Rick Martel walking out on Tito Santana at WrestleMania V. I love the way the story was told because no one saw it coming. It was supposed to be Strike Force's triumphant return after losing the tag team titles the year before at WrestleMania IV. Tully Blanchard ducked out of the way of Tito's flying forearm and Tito wound up hitting Martel, knocking him out of the ring. At that point, you never really saw the good guys have a miscue like that. When Martel got back on the apron, Tito reached for him and Martel walked away at first, then said 'forget this' and walked back to the dressing room, leaving Tito in a handicap match. At first, I don't think anyone thought Rick Martel would make a good heel because he was always Mr Nice Guy, but he went on to have a great run as a heel and Tito never forgave him because every year in Royal Rumbles after that, Tito always went right for Martel. Martel should've been IC champ, but never got the opportunity.

Glenn Cavazzi

'Head Over Heels, or: Not At Face Value'

An analysis on why heels are cheered over babyfaces in professional wrestling.

I present to you a man who is a cheater, a thief, and a liar. He looks out only for himself and willingly manipulates others for personal gain. This man is cocky, mean-spirited, treacherous and often quite nasty if not downright evil. Would you praise this man?

In the world of professional wrestling, where anything can happen even though everything is scripted and the extensive rule book is thrown out at the first drop of a referee, it isn't a stretch of the imagination for that to be true.

There is a very basic concept that has been driven into the minds of every human being since childhood: support the good guys in their fight against the bad ones. The heroes are the ones that we should root for, not the villains. After all, they represent everything that we should drive to be. Contrary to the villains, these men and women are honourable and thoughtful with a lot of determination and heart. Unfortunately, they can also be boring.

As much as sports entertainment would like to control the fans to ensure that the babyfaces are cheered and the heels are booed, keeping everything black and white, it is not immune from the grey areas that life presents to us. Sometimes, the heels just end up being the fan favourites.

Why is that? How can these deplorable people be the ones that get more of a reaction from the audience? Your mileage may vary on the details, but in general, there are four primary explanations for this occurrence.

First and foremost, villains are the driving force of stories. Without conflict, there is no purpose. Romance stories are about the courting process, not the 'happily ever after'. Comedies are about the struggles of stupidity. Action stories revolve around the hero trying to stop the villain. Typically, if a babyface wrestles a babyface, there is no story other than that both men want to win a match. The feuds that have more substance almost always have a villain in them to build around.

One of the biggest ways to achieve this in professional wrestling is to create a storyline wherein a heel is the champion and on top of the company. It is then up to various babyfaces to attempt to be the one to stop him and put his reign of tyranny to an end. Conversely, if the champion is a babyface, the storyline typically involves the heel being a thorn in his side and attacking him. In both situations, the focal point is the heel's perspective. Giving that spotlight to the villain allows for a wider margin that he will be the one who is more over with the crowd. Popularity tends to spread and more screen time means more of a chance for popularity to begin with.

When crafting a story, it's important to not just have a 'what', but also a 'why'. We know what the heel is doing, but we also need to give him a driving force to explain his actions. To beef things up, the heel is given a huge dose of character development, which boosts his ability to be interesting to the audience.

Simply put, a more interesting character is always going to connect with the audience easier than one who is bland. When we get to know more about the person, we identify with them and can follow their journey. There is room to grow and flexibility too, whereas with many babyfaces, the characters need to be so set in their ways and already so self-actualised that they are stuck on repeat mode. When a heel has a microphone, you never know what he is going to say, but when a babyface is holding the stick, you can bet your house that the same old retired promo on respect and fighting against the odds is going to come out.

Babyfaces are often stripped of character out of fear that they will be seen as villainous if they do anything but act like a Boy Scout. However, the broken record of humility and eating your vegetables causes a lot of people to tune out. Instead, the heels are the ones that inject some life back into things.

Stand-out characters on television shows are often the flawed ones that are a bit adversarial to the rest of the cast. The majority of the most popular superheroes are the ones that have a heel-like edge to them, such as Spider-Man's mockery of his foes, Batman's troubled psyche and Wolverine's brash attitude. In wrestling, this is no different. The more interesting the character, the more likely the fans will become emotionally invested in them. When babyfaces appear as cardboard cutouts with the personality of a brick wall, it's only natural for heels to capture the attention.

Branching off on the characterisation aspect, another reason that cannot be ignored for why heels can be cheered more than faces is the 'bad boy' effect. This is a phenomenon in relationships where someone is attracted to someone else because they represent something of a risk. For some, it is the mere fact that they are different that draws them in. Others are more interested in the challenge of changing the individual and the potential redemption that can happen.

This can be taken in a romantic sense, as a fan can be attracted to a heel in a sexual way and cheer them because of this, or it can be more of a hero-worship perspective. A popular phrase to describe the James Bond character is that 'women want to be with him and men want to be him'. If a babyface has the personality of a wet dishcloth but a heel is considered cool, many men will cheer the heel because that is the type of personality that they would rather be. When you question people if they'd prefer to have popularity and fame over integrity and loyalty, most people think the former is more glamorous and lust for that instead. Nice guys finish last, after all.

Many heels only remain popular after transitioning to a babyface role if they continue to have these same aspects. Shawn Michaels and Triple H are very much still their D-Generation X counterparts. The Undertaker still refers to taking souls and essentially killing his opponents. The only difference between 'Stone Cold' Steve Austin's character as a heel and a babyface was the alignment of the person that he was currently facing at the time. He still maintained the cursing, beer-drinking, ass-whooping traits in both roles.

Lastly, the draw of the bad boy is predominantly a reflection of the urge to rebel, which is something that some wrestling fans crave. Further diving into the popularity of Steve Austin, one of the main reasons for his success was the angle of sticking it to your boss. Fans could relate to this, as they had the same feelings about their own respective bosses in real life. Within the world of professional wrestling, there is an understood boss that the fans bow down to – the members of the creative writing team. We are told to cheer a certain person and expected to go along with the rules.

But sometimes, it's more fun to break those rules. Certain audiences are notorious for going in the opposite route from what is expected of them. If you are in Philadelphia, Chicago or New York, you can expect a pure-as-white Rey Mysterio to be booed while a conniving heathen like Edge will receive a standing ovation. In some instances, a heel being cheered can just boil down to reverse psychology. If you tell us to do one thing, we might want to do another.

By no means does this translate to babyfaces being pointless in comparison. If professional wrestling only had heels, the saturation of the same negative atmosphere would be overkill. You can't have a light without a dark to stick in it, but without that light, you're blind.

Many times, it is quite literally a slap in the face when a heel is cheered. But as history has shown us with the likes of those mentioned above as well as 'Rowdy' Roddy Piper, Chris Jericho, Mick Foley and others, it can often lead to the best babyface turns in history.

The next time you find yourself rooting for a heel, ask yourself whether any of these reasons apply to you. Is this a situation where you're supporting a heel because they are legitimately more entertaining to you, you find them more interesting and you fulfil your fantasies by joining their side? Or is it perhaps that his opponent is a face that only a mother could love?

Anthony Mango is the owner-operator of the wrestling website Smark Out Moment, a featured columnist on Bleacher Report and consultant for the independent wrestling organisation Old Time Wrestling.

Summer of 2003 WWE: In my hometown of Detroit, MI at a *SmackDown* taping I was scheduled to wrestle Matt Hardy. I was excited because I really enjoyed working with Matt and I was happy to be performing at the Joe Louis Arena. The office called me the morning of the show informing me that I would be wrestling Brock Lesnar instead. And they wanted to know if my mother could be part of the match.

At this point, Brock had just turned heel, maybe three weeks before. The problem was, he was still getting face reactions from the audience. WWE saw an opportunity to get a little more steam on Brock by having him beat the shit out of me in my home town in front of my mom. Plus the juxtaposition was too good to pass up: he's a 300-pound gorilla and I'm a 150 skinny weakling…with only one fucking leg.

I won't go into details but if you haven't seen the match, please YouTube it. This was the match that prompted WWE to move forward with their more family friendly PG initiative. It was that violent.

This next story is the only time I cried while watching professional wrestling. I may get the names or the exact situation wrong because I was eight years old and it was such a traumatic experience.

Here's what I remember: Fall of 1991. I was in my family's basement watching WCW. Barry Windham comes to the ring to cut a promo on how he can't compete at that night's event or some future event because of his broken hand, which has a cast on it. I remember feeling legitimately bad for Barry. You could tell that not being able to compete pained him greatly. Also please keep in mind that I had a cast on my leg going on three months. This is before the doctors discovered the cancerous tumour on my femur and were just treating the break in my leg as a regular, good ol' fashioned broken leg.

So while Barry's explaining how sorry he is that he can't compete, that no good son of a bitch Arn Anderson decides to interrupt him. Arn verbally berates him, which I thought was totally unfair and unnecessary. I mean the poor guy wants to compete but the doctors wouldn't clear him. He's just trying to do the right thing and explain the situation to the good, hard-working fans of WCW. Anyway, after some back and forth between the two, Arn cheap shots Barry. BAM! Barry goes down. This is awful; I mean the guy isn't even supposed to be in the ring yet he's getting laid out. But the worst was yet to come.

Arn starts stomping the holy hell out of Barry's cast. I literally feel Barry's pain. Arn will not stop the assault. Barry's cast breaks into a million pieces, leaving his raw, broken hand exposed…

At this point I hop upstairs as fast as I can with tears streaming down my face. My mother is cooking dinner in the kitchen. I try to explain what just happened to my mom. She tells me that wrestling is fake, I tell her that I know it is but this just happened to be real. Very real. I'm inconsolable. I was traumatised to the point where I didn't watch WCW until 1996.

Zach Gowen

4
As The Heel Turns – Make A List

Wild Adriatic drummer Mateo Vosganian's top five all-time heels

1. Bobby Heenan
2. Sgt. Slaughter
3. Ted DiBiase
4. Kane
5. Steve Austin

Five terrible heel runs by notable faces

1. Jimmy 'Superfly' Snuka (WWE)
2. 'Hacksaw' Jim Duggan (WCW)
3. Goldberg (New Blood)
4. DDP (WWE)
5. The Artist Formerly Known as Prince Iaukea (WCW)

Authors' heel turn – five guys pushed too much
1. Mark Henry
2. Shawn Michaels
3. Ryback
4. Bobby Lashley
5. 'Cowboy' Bob Orton

Sam Roberts, Opie & Anthony producer's top five heels ever
1. Vince McMahon
2. Roddy Piper
3. Ric Flair
4. Ted DiBiase
5. Rick Rude

Ten heels with better mic skills than 'Big Poppa Pump' Scott Steiner
1. Jake 'The Snake' Roberts
2. Bobby 'The Brain' Heenan
3. 'Macho Man' Randy Savage
4. Ric Flair
5. 'Rowdy' Roddy Piper
6. 'Stone Cold' Steve Austin
7. Triple H
8. Bam Bam Bigelow
9. Slick
10. Bret Hart

Ten heel teams that went the way of Elmwood Dodgeball
1. The Highlanders
2. The Heart Throbs
3. The Dicks
4. The Hart Dynasty
5. Deuce and Domino

6 Cryme Tyme
  7 LOD 2000
  8 The Spirit Squad
  9 New Midnight Express
 10 La Resistance

Heels on banana peels – ten bad guys who dropped the ball
  1 The Giant
  2 Dennis Rodman
  3 Spanky
  4 Billy Kidman
  5 Vampiro
  6 Ryback
  7 Bobby Lashley
  8 Tyson Tomko
  9 Sting
 10 Linda McMahon for Senate

Alphabet City
   MVP
   CM Punk
   JJ Dillion
   IRS
   HHH
   JBL
   HBK
   JTG
   Booker T
   Big Daddy V
   PMS

Ten wrestlers who did a better heel turn than Maven
  1 Rick Martel
  2 Shawn Michaels

3 Sgt. Slaughter
   4 The Rock
   5 Al Snow
   6 Danny Davis
   7 Edge
   8 Michael Cole
   9 Eugene
  10 David Flair

Authors' heel turn – ten over-rated Superstars
   1 Undertaker
   2 Shawn Michaels
   3 Triple H
   4 Bret Hart
   5 Big Show
   6 Trish Stratus
   7 Kane
   8 Jerry Lawler
   9 Sgt. Slaughter
  10 The Rock

Heel today, gone tomorrow – ten bad guys we lost too soon
   1 'Ravishing' Rick Rude
   2 Brian Pillman
   3 Curt Hennig
   4 Eddie Guerrero
   5 Randy Savage
   6 Big John Studd
   7 Andre the Giant
   8 Umaga
   9 Adrian Adonis
  10 Earthquake

Three-man madness
1. Fabulous Freebirds
2. Demolition
3. The Shield
4. The Holly Cousins
5. Mean Street Posse
6. The Mexicools
7. Blue World Order (bWo)
8. The Brood
9. The Legacy
10. The Wyatt Family

Ten bad guys who never won the world title
1. Scott Hall
2. 'Rowdy' Roddy Piper
3. Gorgeous George
4. The Original Sheik
5. King Kong Bundy
6. Davey Boy Smith
7. Brian Pillman
8. Butch Reed
9. Gorilla Monsoon
10. Honky Tonk Man

Ten larger-than-life baddies
1. Andre the Giant
2. King Kong Bundy
3. Vader
4. King Mabel
5. Big John Studd
6. Sycho Sid
7. Giant Gonzalez
8. Kamala
9. The Giant
10. Earthquake

The heel show within a show
1. Piper's Pit
2. The Brother Love Show
3. A Flair For The Gold
4. Highlight Reel
5. VIP Lounge
6. King's Court
7. The Cutting Edge
8. Carlito's Cabana
9. The Funeral Parlor
10. Miz TV

Real-life foreign objects
1. Iron Sheik
2. Dino Bravo
3. Alberto Del Rio
4. Ivan Koloff
5. Ludvig Borga
6. Boris Zhukov
7. Antonio Cesaro
8. Mr Fuji
9. Muhammad Hassan
10. Mr Saito

Ten heel turns we didn't see coming
1. Hulk Hogan creates the nWo
2. Andre the Giant turns on the Hulkster on Piper's Pit
3. Randy Savage breaks up the Mega Powers
4. Billy Kidman calls out Hulk Hogan on WCW
5. Triple H turns on DX at WrestleMania XXV
6. The Rock joins The Corporation
7. Sgt. Slaughter turns on the USA
8. Paul Bearer turns on The Undertaker
9. Paul Orndorff turns on Hogan
10. Scott Steiner turns on Rick Steiner

5
Heel Of Fame – These Baddies Should Be Enshrined Somewhere

THERE is a Pro Wrestling Hall of Fame in Amsterdam, NY. Every year, the day before WrestleMania, World Wrestling Entertainment (WWE) holds its own Hall induction ceremony honouring greats from the past (most recently Mick Foley and Bruno Sammartino to name two), and past cheap pop participants who have no real place in squared circle legacy (Drew Carey? Pete Rose? Really?).

Those respective halls are of note, but we would argue there should be an entire wing devoted to heels. Perhaps Cooperstown could open this aforementioned section by inducting baseball baddies like Roger Clemens or Barry Bonds, and then spin-off a wrestling wing within the wing.

Since that action is a pipe dream, we're going to give villains a fictional enshrinement in the pages that follow. Here are some baddies who deserve to be immortalised forever – even if it's just in this book. Below we'll provide a quote that would go on the individual or stable's plaque, notable accomplishments, and – in a literal tip of the cap to Cooperstown – which 'hat' they would go in the Heel Hall with (i.e. WWE, WCW, or ECW).

Hopefully, Wade Boggs isn't reading this. If he is, he may want to change his cap. Tampa Bay? Really? Anyway, here are just a few in no particular order or odour.

Adrian Adonis aka Keith A. Franke
'He gave Flower Power new meaning.'
Cap: WWE
WWE Tag Team Champion
AWA World Tag Team Champion
NWA Americas Heavyweight Champion

'The Model' Rick Martel
'Suck it, Cheryl Tiegs.'
Cap: WWE
WWE Tag Team Champion
WCW Television Champion
AWA World Heavyweight Champion

Bad News Brown
'No news was good news with Bad News.'
Cap: WWE
WrestleMania Battle Royal Winner
1976 Olympic Games bronze medallist, Judo

The Undertaker
'WrestleMania winning streak rollin' 'til retirement.'
Cap: WWE
WWE Champion
WWE World Heavyweight Champion
WWE Tag Team Champion
2007 Royal Rumble Winner
Limp Bizkit fan

Jake 'The Snake' Roberts
'Beyond the Mat wasn't his finest hour.'
Cap: WWE
The Snake Pit host
NWA National Television Champ

6
Drop-kicktionary

PROFESSIONAL wrestling has a language all to itself. Many times you will hear these words on weekly television episodes or during pay-per-views. Other times you will hear them used frequently by insiders and mostly by wrestling fans themselves. It should also be noted that knowledge of this glossary or lack thereof is the difference between being a midcarder on *Sunday Night Heat* or being in the main event at WrestleMania.

> When I was ten years old I saw Johnny Valentine turn heel against Wilbur Snyder in Chicago. I haven't seen anything since that was nearly as believable!
>
> **'Leaping' Lanny Poffo**

Angle: A fictional storyline or plot that involves one or several wrestlers/personalities that leads up to a match or series of matches. Two of the most successful angles in the history of professional wrestling were the nWo invasion in WCW and the WWE Attitude Era feud between 'Stone Cold' Steve Austin and the chairman Vince McMahon.

Booker: The person in charge of setting up matches, setting up angles and pre-determining the winners and losers.

Bump: This is when a wrestler hits the mat or ground or in some cases the Spanish announce booth.

Dark match: Usually an opening match that happens before the actual televised event and features up and coming stars, or after a televised event that features main-event talent in order to help promote the show and put more behinds in the seats.

Foreign object: An object such as a chair or brass knuckles that is illegal to use during a wrestling match. During the late 1990s ECW (Extreme Championship Wrestling) glorified the use of foreign objects, which included everything and the kitchen sink. This type of wrestling, that was popularised by the stiff legal use of household appliances and other props, became better known as hardcore wrestling.

Green: Often a word used to describe an inexperienced wrestler who is prone to make mistakes.

Heat: A negative reaction that a wrestler or personality gets from either the fans or other talent within the company.

Humanoids: Term often used by manager turned broadcast journalist Bobby 'The Brain' Heenan to describe wrestling fans or other wrestlers that he deemed to be unintelligent.

Throughout the 1980s and 90s wrestling fans were also often referred to by the Hall of Famer as being 'ham-and-eggers'.

Jobber: A wrestler whose sole purpose is to lose to other better-known wrestlers.

Also known as enhancement talent, this particular breed of wrestler essentially gets paid to lose on a nightly basis.

Jumping ship: Term used to describe when a wrestler has switched to another promotion.

Promo: Interview made by a wrestler or personality that is in character and is used to advance a storyline. Among the all-time best in the industry at 'cutting a promo' are The Rock, 'Macho Man' Randy Savage and 'Stone Cold' Steve Austin.

Mid-carder: Wrestler who usually wrestles on the middle of the card and competes for secondary titles. Neither a jobber nor a main eventer.

Heel: The Darth Vader of the wrestling industry. Term used to describe the villain or bad guy.

Face: The good guy. Also known as the babyface.

Hulk up: The no-sell of an opponent's onslaught of manoeuvres, usually an unbelievable comeback by a face wrestler. Named after the legendary comebacks of Hulk Hogan.

Squash: A quick one-sided match meant to make one wrestler look good over another. Usually meant for a monster push and to help a gimmick get over with fans. Many of Bill Goldberg's matches during his memorable undefeated streak in WCW were squash matches used to make him look unstoppable as well as making up for his limited mic skills and charisma.

7
Heel Stables – The Good, The Bad And The Hornswoggle

The Four Horsemen

BIO/RUN: The standard-bearer for all professional wrestling stables, the Horsemen began their dominance in 1986 and forever altered the way rule-breakers were seen and heard all while busting the balls (literally how many Flair junk punches can one guy withstand?) of NWA golden boys Dusty Rhodes, Magnum T.A. and the Rock 'n' Roll Express.

While the original quartet consisted of Ric Flair, Tully Blanchard and Arn and Ole Anderson, over the years the fourth spot soon became a hotbed for up and coming baddies looking to shine in the bright lights such as Lex Luger, Sid Vicious and Barry Windham.

They were trend-setters who helped usher in the era of heel stables that still resonates to this day.

GREATEST MOMENT: In 1988 when Barry Windham began flashing the four-fingered symbol of excellence the Horsemen saw their greatest success in the form of capturing all the major NWA straps at one time, with Flair as the World Heavyweight Champion, Windham as the United States Champion and Arn and Tully as the World Tag Champions. The Horsemen defined greatness, dominance and yes even several years later we give them a mulligan for allowing Mongo McMichael to become a card-carrying member.

BEST: The obvious choice being Ric Flair whose 289 World Championships allow him to be the only Team Package member to reside atop the Mount Rushmore of wrestling. However, the hardest-working member of the Horsemen was Flair's trusted confidant Arn Anderson. Billed as the enforcer he not only talked the talk but he also spinning-spine-busted his way as the most recognised star among stars in the Horsemen stable.

WORST: In 1993 the group was down to three official members and with Paul Roma in the three hole it is sure to be considered the darkest moment in Horsemen lore, but for an ill-fated incident months later involving Sid Vicious and a pair of scissors.

MEMBERS: Ric Flair, Arn Anderson, Ole Anderson, Tully Blanchard, James J. Dillion, Lex Luger, Sting, Brian Pillman, Dean Malenko, Chris Benoit, Sid Vicious, Curt Hennig, Paul Roma, Barry Windham, Jeff Jarrett, Steve 'Mongo' McMichael.

D-Generation X

BIO/RUN: They were a direct product of WWE's Attitude Era. Crude and controversial, the DX army has been running strong since late in the last century. With their disregard for authority and obnoxiously rude 'Suck it' chants the rebellious gang led by Shawn Michaels and Hunter Hearst Helmsley have milked more merchandise out of a simple crotch chop than any other team in sports entertainment history. What once was entertaining in-your-face programming soon became an unwatchable glowstick-tossing event geared toward the now kid-friendly WWE fan base.

GREATEST MOMENT: On 28 April 1998, in the midst of the Monday Night Wars, DX members showed up to a WCW event in Norfolk, Virginia, dressed in their best Hogan's Heroes camouflage and proceed to berate the *Nitro* product through the use of their bullhorn and a jeep that looked like it came straight off the set of *M.A.S.H.*

The move was not only historic but it also proved that the group would continue to push the envelope at any cost.

BEST: Despite their sophomoric pranks and provocative language the group has for the better part of their existence been well received by most fans. Much like Austin and The Rock, DX dabbled in the sort of grey area and therefore breaking the rules was seen as a great way to get over with the fans.

That being said the most heat on the group was during the build-up to WrestleMania XIV when they enlisted the services of boxing great 'Iron' Mike Tyson who served as the group's special enforcer. Many years later they inducted the baddest man on the planet into the Liberace-less WWE Hall of Fame Celebrity Wing.

WORST: In 2009, after 'suing' them for emotional and physical distress, Hornswoggle was named the first and only ever DX mascot.

MEMBERS: Triple H, Shawn Michaels, Rick Rude, Chyna, New Age Outlaws (Road Dogg and Billy Gunn), X-Pac, Hornswoggle, Mike Tyson.

Nexus

BIO/RUN: They breathed new life into a promotion that was in need of a new age in pro wrestling. After the first season of NXT wrapped up the eight existing rookies joined forces and set their sights on the entire World Wrestling Entertainment roster. Although their main target was John Cena, who later reluctantly became a member of the group, they also set sights on other notable personalities such as Bret Hart, Vince McMahon and Ricky 'The Dragon' Steamboat. Whether led by Wade Barrett or CM Punk the super-group of upstarts made an immediate and dominating impact never to be forgotten.

GREATEST MOMENT: In devastating fashion the Nexus made their debut and left Cena and the entire *Raw* set a battered mess of chaos and devastation. You are either Nexus or you're against us!

BEST: Although the group has come and gone the current roster of WWE stars is filled with its share of Nexus-influenced superstars. Barrett is a former Intercontinental Champion and if the faces of Bray Wyatt, Curtis Axel and Ryback look familiar then picture them with the group's trademark black and yellow armband.

WORST: During their initial beat-down on Cena and the *Raw* crew, Daniel Bryan took the liberty to strangle ring announcer Justin Roberts with his necktie leading to his release from the company as it was deemed too violent for their TV-PG rated television show.

MEMBERS: Wade Barrett, David Otunga, Michael McGillicutty, Michael Tarver, Husky Harris, Skip Sheffield, Darren Young, Heath Slater, CM Punk, Justin Gabriel, John Cena, Daniel Bryan, Mason Ryan.

Hart Foundation

BIO/RUN: Over two decades of dominance for this group that was originally a tag team back in the 1980s led by Jimmy Hart and some years later toward the end of the 1990s the re-formation of the Foundation occurred as the rule-breaking Bret Hart waged war on the United States with his pro-Canadian family members backing his every move.

GREATEST MOMENT: At the Calgary Saddledome the Hart Foundation defeated 'Stone Cold' Steve Austin, Goldust, the Legion of Doom and Ken Shamrock during an In Your House Pay-Per-View. Owen rolled up the Rattlesnake for the win, which culminated in an in-ring celebration between several members of the Hart family.

BEST: At one time they held the WWE Championship, Intercontinental Championship, European Championship, and Tag Team Championship.

WORST: In late 1997 Brian Pillman was found dead on the day of In Your House: Badd Blood, and one month later at the company's next pay-per-view event Bret Hart would lose the WWE Championship after the now infamous Montreal Screwjob.

MEMBERS: Bret Hart, Jim 'The Anvil' Neidhart, Davey Boy Smith, Jimmy Hart, Brian Pillman, Owen Hart.

Dudley Boyz

BIO/RUN: If you follow the signs to Parts Unknown somewhere in between South Philadelphia and New Rochelle, New York, you will find Dudleyville. During the late 1990s the Dudleys were making a name for themselves as the most hardcore and ruthless family in wrestling. Led by D-Von and Bubba Ray, the Dudleys transformed into a team that almost single-handedly revolutionised the tag team industry.

GREATEST MOMENT: With the help of flaming tables and the patented Dudley Death Drop the duo won a record-breaking 23 Tag Team Championships.

BEST: They are the only team to ever win the ECW, WCW and WWE World Tag Team Championships.

WORST: The fact that they left Dances With Dudley in ECW is still one of wrestling's greatest mysteries.

MEMBERS: Big Dick Dudley, Buh Buh Ray Dudley (Bubba Ray Dudley), D-Von Dudley, Dances With Dudley, Dudley Dudley, Sign Guy Dudley, Spike Dudley, Snot Dudley, Chubby Dudley.

Heenan Family

BIO/RUN: The main target for this Heenan-led group, which he liked to refer to as his 'Family', was the WWE Champion Hulk Hogan. Beginning in the

AWA, the Brain soon brought his smarts to the northeast and helped lead rule-breakers against the good guys of the WWE. He was there when Big John Studd attempted to slam the eighth wonder of the world in a bodyslam challenge at WrestleMania I and he was front and centre when his client King Kong Bundy lost to the Hulkster a year later in a blue steel cage (they need to bring that back by the way). His greatest acquisition was recruiting Andre the Giant to fight Hogan in front of 93,000 fans at the third installment of the grandest stage of them all. Heenan's Family members were a who's who of wrestling bad guy royalty that helped make the manager a lot of money. Now, if we can only get one of those sequined Brain shirts on eBay…

GREATEST MOMENT: Perhaps the greatest moment during the Heenan regime was when the Brain grabbed on to a leg and helped Rick Rude defeat the Ultimate Warrior for the Intercontinental Championship.

BEST: Sure the Rude win was great but these other championships were just as sweet: The Brain Busters were Tag Team Champions under Heenan's watch while Mr Perfect saw his greatest success during his time with the Brain. Ric Flair won two WWE Championships led by the greatest broadcast journalist in wrestling history.

WORST: With the Brooklyn Brawler in his corner, Bobby Heenan lost to the Red Rooster at WrestleMania V.

MEMBERS: Bobby 'The Brain' Heenan, Big John Studd, Ken Patera, Haku, Andre the Giant, King Kong Bundy, Mr Wonderful Paul Orndorff, Ravishing Rick Rude, The Brain Busters (Tully Blanchard and Arn Anderson), Mr Perfect, Ric Flair, The Missing Link, Adrian Adonis, Buddy Rose, King Harley Race, Hercules, The Brooklyn Brawler, The Islanders, Barbarian, The Red Rooster.

Nation of Domination

BIO/RUN: Starting off first as a militant group hell-bent on gaining equality by any means, the Nation soon transformed its vision and began to set its sights on WWE Championship gold. Leadership, which was at first helmed by the former Ron Simmons, was soon under The Rock's influence and from there the Nation flourished to a certain degree.

GREATEST MOMENT: In December 1997 The Rock was awarded the Intercontinental Championship after Steve Austin refused to defend it, giving the Nation its first and only title-holder in its existence.

BEST: During the Nation's transformation from Faarooq to The Rock, Nation member Kama Mustafa was able to loosen up a bit which allowed for his inner pimp to shine and soon the Godfather and his Ho-train were making local stops at WWE events all over the country.

WORST: They spent too much time chasing down Ahmed Johnson and less time focusing on the real prize of complete and utter domination of the WWE and Monday night television.

MEMBERS: Faarooq, Rocky Maivia, Owen Hart, Crush, Savio Vega, D'Lo Brown, PG13 (JC Ice and Wolfie D), Kama Mustafa, Ahmed Johnson, Mark Henry, Clarence Mason.

nWo

Considered to be the greatest stable, angle and moment of all time. It began when Scott Hall left WWE and brought his talents to WCW. Soon joined by his Kliq buddy Kevin Nash, the two Outsiders claimed that they were taking over the company with help from a mystery partner. They challenged three of WCW's greatest stars – Sting, Lex Luger and Randy Savage. In the most amazing swerve of all time Hulk Hogan was revealed to be the mystery partner and just like that the new world order of wrestling was born.

The bad-guy beard-growing Hulkster said it best the night he turned his back on his legion of fans, 'If it wasn't for Hulk Hogan Eric Bischoff would be still selling meat from a truck in Minneapolis!' The stage was set and soon the three outlaws were attacking anyone and anything associated with WCW. They attacked faces and heels and the hostile takeover was in full effect once they began to add members week after week. You were glued to your television every week at 7.57pm just to see what the black and white were going to do next. Let's be honest, they even had a fake Sting in their group. They dominated for a good year and a half and while WCW was WWE's behind it was Ted Turner getting the last laugh as he continued to win the Monday night rating war guided by the renegade nWo group.

GREATEST MOMENT: The initial turn which saw Hogan riding in on his white horse a sure bet to dispose of all the wrong-doing that the Outsiders were perpetrating and out of nowhere the leg drop heard round the world. Hogan's speech was priceless and the littered ring only added fuel to the fire.

BEST: One of the coolest moments during the nWo angle was when the group began spray-painting its logo on stuff including the backs of beaten wrestlers. Immortalised forever will be the sight of 'Hollywood' Hulk Hogan spraying nWo on the prestigious World Heavyweight Championship belt.

WORST: As bad as it was watching Hogan running around in the classic tees, the watered-down WWE version, which included HBK and Booker T, was simply the worst and thankfully it didn't last too long.

MEMBERS: 'Hollywood' Hulk Hogan, Kevin Nash, Scott Hall, Ted DiBiase, The Giant, Fake Sting, Syxx,

Vincent, Elizabeth, Eric Bischoff, Nick Patrick, Buff Bagwell, V.K. Wallstreet, Big Bubba Rogers, Masahiro Chono, Scott Norton, Randy Savage, Konnan, Rick Rude, Dusty Rhodes, Dennis Rodman, Scott Steiner, Brian Adams, Bret Hart, The Disciple, Horace Hogan, Stevie Ray, Sting, Lex Luger, Disco Inferno, David Flair, Jeff Jarrett, The Harris Brothers, Booker T, Shawn Michaels.

Dungeon of Doom

BIO/RUN: Created for the sole purpose of destroying and ridding World Championship Wrestling of everything good it represented, in other words beginning and ending with Hulkamania.

GREATEST MOMENT: The Giant comes back from getting tossed off the roof of the arena during a monster truck match and somehow wins against Hulk Hogan on his debut.

BEST: The Giant's clean pin victory over Ric Flair on *Nitro* helped elevate him to main event status.

WORST: Someone in the back decided it was a good idea to give Tiny Lister another 15 minutes in the wrestling spotlight – can you say box office blunder?

MEMBERS: The Master, Taskmaster Kevin Sullivan, Kamala, The Shark, Zodiac, Big Van Vader, Meng,

The Giant, The Yeti, Lex Luger, Jimmy Hart, One Man Gang, Hugh Morrus, Barbarian, Loch Ness, Z-Gangsta, The Ultimate Solution, Maxx, Big Bubba, Konnan, The Leprechaun.

The Fabulous Freebirds

BIO/RUN: Ahead of their time, the Freebirds were brought together way back in 1979 and this dangerous threesome from Atlanta, Georgia, formed a bond built on showmanship and dirty rule-breaking unseen before or since. With a gang-like mentality the three 'birds held titles in the NWA, World Class Championship Wrestling and the UWF. Not only did they break the rules but they made them as well when they invented what is known as the 'Freebird Rule' which is when any two people of the stable can defend the tag team titles. Through various promotions the trio had a reputation for beating people up and causing hell whenever and with whomever they liked.

GREATEST MOMENT: They captured the World Class Six Man Championship, becoming the first team to do so and in an instant began one of the bloodiest feuds in wrestling history with the Von Erich family. During the rivalry the teams traded the belts at least ten times.

BEST: Helping to redefine the industry as only they can, the group's leader Michael 'PS' Hayes became the first wrestling star to ever record his own entrance theme, which was titled 'Bad Street USA'.

WORST: During a WCW run the Freebirds (the team of Michael Hayes and Jimmy Garvin) introduced a masked wrestler by the name of Fantasia who later changed his name to Badstreet. Whatever the hell his name was he bore a close resemblance to Brad Armstrong and with or without Armstrong this incarnation of the Freebirds was definitely lacking the group's trademark rebellious attitude and southern charm.

MEMBERS: Michael Hayes, Terry Gordy, Buddy Roberts, Jimmy 'Jam' Garvin, Badstreet.

8
Name That Tune – Heel Edition

JAKE 'The Snake' Roberts is arguably the best heel the modern era of wrestling ever saw. Not only did the moustachioed star hold his own in the ring – his DDT is literally the only DDT worth mentioning in our book – but his impeccable mic skills in pre-match promos, The Snake Pit, and interviews with 'Mean' Gene Okerlund, are what made him a legend.

Triple H may be known as the 'cerebral assassin' but it was Roberts who really lived up to that moniker – getting inside his opponents' heads with his sharp tongue, wit, and snake in a bag. He was a badass – entering the ring with Damien, and slowly walking into the ring with a chip on his shoulder.

The one thing Roberts didn't have, however, was a strong entrance theme. The perennial bad guy needed a theme song worthy of his talents, but instead, got a song that sounds like a *Miami Vice* knock-off tune. Heavy on synthesisers and anything the probably coked-out 1980s music producers could throw in, the lead-in didn't match the intenseness Roberts had in and out of the ring. The Snake warranted a theme more in line with Sycho Sid Vicious, whose theme song was part horror movie/part Thomas Dolby and all badass.

Having said that, more times than not the badder the heel, the worse their entrance music has been. Sure, there are exceptions to that bold statement, but they're few and far between. The Undertaker's theme – particularly the version by Ministry – is arguably the best in the history of heel entrance music. From the gong to the music that follows it, the production is the perfect soundtrack to the Phenom's persona, look and legacy.

Chris Benoit also had a solid entrance song. While he has been banished from WWE programming following his apparent murder-suicide (rightfully so), you can't take away how good the Crippler's use of fellow Canucks' Our Lady Peace's 'Whatever' was. The song was the perfect way to introduce the go-for-broke wrestler who had paid his dues by any means necessary to make it in the business.

Whereas Benoit went with Our Lady Peace, Triple H has enjoyed a nice partnership with Lemmy and Motorhead. 'Time to Play the Game' is a great way to get instant heat whenever it hits out of the speakers whenever Hunter is a heel or arguably when he turns babyface. Love him or hate him, the song just works and matches the intensity the grappler brings to the ring – spitting water and all.

Unlike Benoit and Triple H, Ted DiBiase sang his own song – well sort of. Backed by wannabe Supremes chanting 'Money, Money, Money…' the Million Dollar Man uttered his catchphrases like 'everyone's got a price' and it just worked. It set the tone right out of the gate for the Trump-minded villain and matched perfectly with the 1980s 'Greed is Good' sentiment.

Sometimes good themes don't need to have lyrics. 'Stone Cold' Steve Austin's 'glass-breaking' ditty sent fans off the rails. Once you would hear the glass breaking, fans at the arena would be as giddy as Catholic schoolgirls on their lunch hour. Sure, Stone Cold was mostly a face, but you can't deny this track.

Ditto for Goldust, who always made a grand impression with his 'Shattered Dreams' intro. From the letterboxed video montage to the monumental instrumental theme, his overall entrance is hard to beat.

The all-instrumental nWo theme with its 'new… new…New World Order' opening always resonated against common sense. The same can be said with 'Cool, Cocky and Bad' which in no way should have worked for the Honky Tonk Man but it does because he has made a career out of selling his persona to grand effect.

But let's move on, because good entrance music for bad guys usually just plain sucks. 'Ravishing' Rick Rude was a stud, who looked like a porn star but wrestled like a superstar. Sadly, his entrance music sounded like a topless vaudeville dancer's theme before she showed off her tatas to some beer-bellied businessmen. The only redeeming thing about the track was how Rude would constantly ask the higher-ups to 'cut the music' so he could flex and make out with a front-row ring rat.

Whereas Rude's intro was schmaltz city, 'The Model' Rick Martel's theme played like something The Dap-Kings would get kicked out of Sharon Jones & The Dap-Kings for playing. Heavy on horns, and not much else, the theme wasn't 'arrogant', but it was excruciatingly stinky.

Similarly, Yokozuna's theme didn't do the grappler justice. With a theme more suitable for a massage table happy ending, this ambient track was a disgrace and a complete conundrum. Yokozuna deserved a better track to wobble into the ring to. At least Yokozuna's theme was an original track.

The 1980s and early 1990s were spent developing characters but not developing distinct themes. For a while all WWE did for entrance music for its superstars was record them with a few lines in the beginning and follow that with some recycled cornball rock track that altogether sounded the same.

Everyone from Vader ('Oh, it's time! It's time! It's Vader time!') to the Legion of Doom ('What a rush!') to New Age Outlaws ('Oh, you didn't know?') followed this blueprint as did WCW's Kronik whose theme started off with what sounded like some German dude just saying the tandem's name.

There is a laundry list of bad theme songs that we could also mention in these pages, but haven't they done enough damage to the business? Aren't you sick of hearing the Four Horsemen theme that basically just sounds like a slowed-down, warped version of Europe's 'The Final Countdown?' Aren't you sick of hearing Shawn Michaels sing 'Sexy Boy' as he enters the ring praying?

We are. For our money, we would rather listen to Randy Savage come in to 'Pomp and Circumstance' or Chris Jericho's 'Break the Walls Down'. Heck, when you throw the aforementioned themes from Vader and Yokozuna in the mix, we would rather listen to Vince McMahon enter the ring repeatedly to 'No Chance'. Will that actually happen? No chance.

9
Bad – We're Drawn That Way

IN movies, television, comic books, and any form of pop culture really, the bad guys rarely win. In the court of public opinion, however, our pop heroes sometimes come a close second to the appeal of a really good baddie. As we've said in this book, the same often holds true with villains in wrestling. But, what if our favourite bad guys from all walks of pop ended up in the squared circle? Hypothetically speaking, how would Darth Vader match up with, say, the Undertaker? Would Heath Ledger's Joker outsmart Sting in the ring? And what about John Malkovich's Mitch Leary character from the 1993 thriller *In the Line of Fire*? How would he do against the likes of ECW's Bill Alfonso or WCW's Kwee Wee?

OK, let's skip that answer because, you know, probably no one cares. But, we think it's an interesting notion so we're taking 25 villains from pop culture and seeing how they would do as top wrestling heels in the ring. Can you smell what The Darth is cookin'?

Darth Vader would be no Dark Helmet in the ring, but his heavy armour would probably weigh him down in any match against a Rey Mysterio Jr. or Sin Cara. Secondly, his gear would make it impossible for him to do a leg drop like the Hulkster or climb to the top rope like Jimmy 'Superfly' Snuka. But, let's be honest the force grip would beat any opponent and possibly even kill them so let's not discount this Sith Lord as a top heel in any company, during any time period, and in any country.

We would suggest entrance music performed by AC/DC, and a feud against that other Vader. This former Jedi, however, wouldn't need a manager to help sway a decision in the ring. His wits and mic skills would kill arena audiences and nerds, who like to make Wookiee impersonations to impress girls, at home.

Can you imagine how innovative the Joker would be in Impact Wrestling, AKA the Company Formerly Known as TNA Wrestling or known to some as No One's Watching Wrestling? It honestly wouldn't matter what incarnation the DC Comic iconic villain would be, it would still resonate especially if the psychopath took on Sting.

Seriously, a clone of Cesar Romero's portrayal would even work. Why? Because Sting has made a career of stealing characters be it The Crow or Heath Ledger's Joker, and it would be cool to have a heel

Even without Damien, Jake the Snake is as slimy and ruthless as they come.

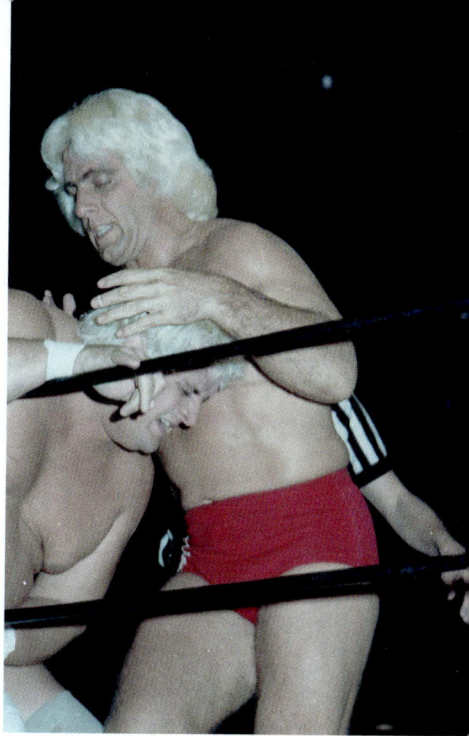

The Nature Boy contemplating his next low blow.

Slick Ric styling and profiling.

Ready to ride Space Mountain.

The late great Eddy Guerrero was always at his best when he was bad.

Textbook eye gouge courtesy of the Funker.

Two of the industry's greatest heels battle it out.

Will this lead to a Dusty finish?

Precursor to the Viper. Cowboy Bob was just as nasty.

Talkin' the talk.

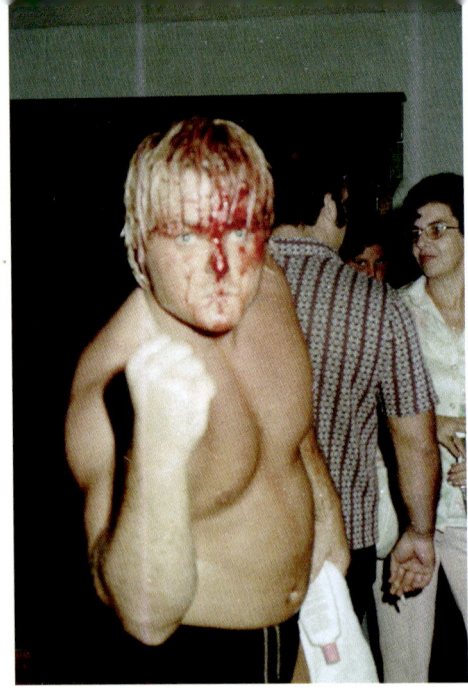
Another day at the office.

A bloody superstar taming the Big Cat.

The Son of a Plumber getting nasty.

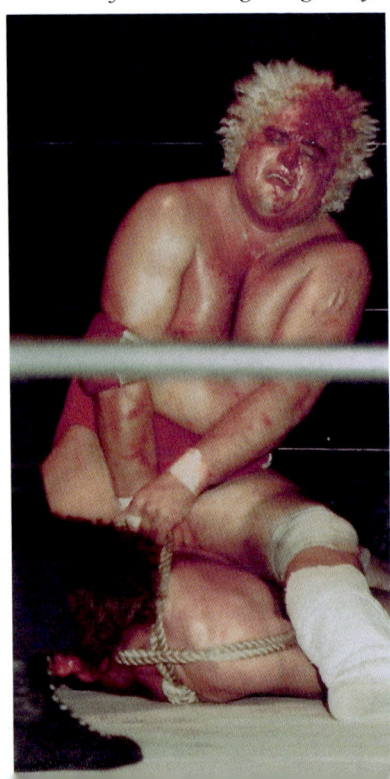

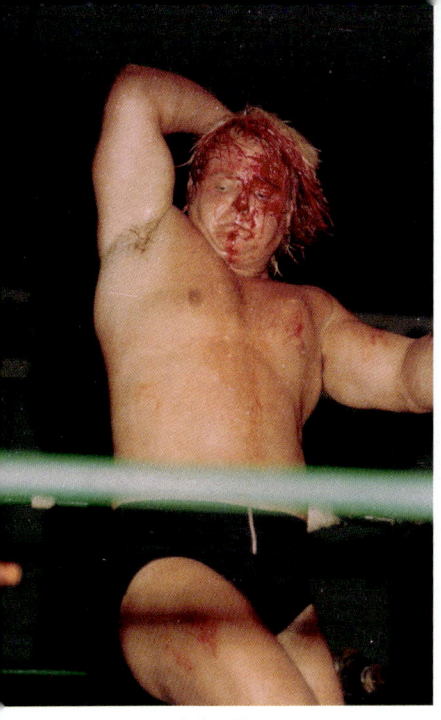

Droppin' the Hammer.

This would have hurt much more if the coconut was involved.

Bray Wyatt learned from the best.

Thunderlips is runnin' wild brother.

Superstar is the man of the hour.

Hey ref is that a choke?

The Hot Rod was also a great barber, just ask the Haiti Kid.

Only the bad guys win.

The Snake is loose.

Please don't try this at home.

The Horsemen.

Pre-Loose Cannon.

Classic Heel spot.

Flair takes the Heel Tour overseas.

Raven is the hardest core.

The Snake contemplates his next DDT victim.

Ata Johnson's Top Five Heels

1. The Rock – The most electrifying, most entertaining, and iconic heel the world has ever seen. I know! I know! But, I'm allowed to be biased since I'm his mom!

2. 'Stone Cold' Steve Austin – A defining heel who would then go on to define the entire Attitude Era as a babyface.

3. Jimmy 'Superfly' Snuka – Before he became the phenom, he was a vicious, believable heel. He put the fear in people! Huge heel!

4. Don Muraco – Cocky, magnetic, go-for-broke arrogance. One of the greats!

5. Pat Patterson – Master of ring psychology as a heel. I witnessed many a match between Patterson and my father 'High Chief' Peter Maivia. Patterson knew how to get the fans in a dither. By the end of the match, people were rioting. It was a scary sight to see in the Cow Palace Arena in San Francisco: two of the rioters were young upstart roughnecks, Samoan brothers Afa and Sika Anoa'i, who would go on to become the dominating, most scariest heels, the Wild Samoans, who became WWE Tag Team Champions and WWE Hall of Famers.

exploit that notion via a series of pranks and promos leading up to a match. On second thought, since Impact Wrestling doesn't have the numbers, reunite the APA and have them play cards with the Joker. Everyone loves a stable, right? Insert a Ron Simmons 'damn' right here.

If one heel could wipe out cartoonish gimmicks and gags in professional wrestling for once and for all, it's Judge Doom of *Who Framed Roger Rabbit?* In the ring, 'the dip' would possibly be a manoeuvre in which he drives his opponent's face to the mat or, better yet, it would just be the dropping of a piano on their head.

A lot of things are recycled in wrestling, but no one has ever had a 'piano' to the face. Big John Studd never took a piano to the face. Neither did The Haiti Kid. Look through YouTube videos, and we highly doubt you would see any results come up for the following: 'piano-to-the-face match'. Judge Doom would reign for years in the WWE today or back in the day.

Speaking of which, we wish the mean-spirited half-man, half-toon from the Toon Town court would have cleaned up the unintentionally comical WWE back in the Doink the Clown era. If anyone deserved 'the dip' it would be that clown.

Agent Smith from *The Matrix* would have an unfair advantage over just about everyone in the wrestling world. For starters, he has super-human strength and is more flexible than a Kardashian sibling after a few Mai Tai rounds. Secondly, he can multiply so opponents might take on multiple versions of the ruthless, soulless, stoic sharp-dressed-man.

But it's not that cut and dried. Mr Smith is a pretty boring guy who looks more like an accountant at a funeral than a top heel. Besides, Trish Stratus gave us more of a rise (albeit in our pants) with her *Matrix* moves. Who needs to see this guy doing it? Anyway, Smith would make a solid mid-carder who could pair up with Fandango in an 'opposites attract' tag-team gimmick. We would love to see them take on The Highlanders for fits and giggles. One thing is for sure, whoever Agent Smith battles would make for solid entertainment that's far less painless and confusing than sitting through the *Matrix* trilogy. Zing!

Alex Cross would accomplish something that no wrestling diva has ever done – she would scare the living daylights out of any male counterpart. We are talking a character far scarier than a Chyna porno who seduces male wrestlers only to take out all her frustrations on them in the ring or the locker room. The stalker gimmick has been done before, but this *Fatal Attraction* bad girl would do it far more justice than DDP. Her finishing move by the way could be hitting her opponents over the head with a stuffed-animal dead rabbit.

Biff Tannen wouldn't be a very compelling bad guy. For starters, his claim to fame is stealing an almanac in a terrible movie sequel and tasting cow manure in the legendary first flick. If that wasn't enough, this *Back to the Future* douche almost raped Marty McFly's mother and comes across as just another dumb jock. A cross between Chris Masters and Festus, Biff would be the Iron Mike Sharpe of his generation if he entered the wrestling world. How bad would he be? Eugene would've outsmarted him.

Hornswoggle is the new Funaki. The pint-sized star has managed to stick around WWE for so many more years that someone had to lose a bet in Vegas. They likely would if *Child's Play* demon Chucky landed in the ring as well. Chucky is a ruthless killer on screen, but he would probably become a novelty heel in any wrestling organisation. How would he even compete with those doll hands?

Sure, the evil-doer would tear up opponents on the microphone with his wisecracks, but could he really compete against Hillbilly Jim back in the day? What about S.D. Jones? We'll lower the bar even further and venture to guess Chucky wouldn't even beat Matilda in a thumb wrestle. Chucky would serve a company far better as a heel manager in the tradition of Captain Lou Albano. Stick him with Tyson Tomko or see if Chuck Palumbo needs work, but leave him out of the squared circle.

Dr Octopus would be at an advantage over most opponents who only have two arms. He would have an advantage over Zach Gowen as well, but that's besides the point. Dr Otto Octavius or 'Doc Ock' is a genius who would be able to not just outsmart an opponent (we can see him taking multiple Ric Flair 'undercarriage' shots with his multiple arms) but physically, he would probably be able to overtake even a bigger guy like Ryback.

But he is not without his flaws. Waving all those limbs around would probably leave the guy winded like a fat kid at a dodgehball game. But, his strengths out-match his weaknesses so sign him up for the nWo 2.0, stat!

Freddy Krueger could probably be a big heel, but only if all the matches took place in the dreamworld. Otherwise, we're guessing he would be screwed. First off, WWE or Impact Wrestling or any indie promoter is never going to allow him to enter the ring with those sharp fingers. Take that away, and leave him to his own devices, and we're guessing Triple H can easily beat him by spewing water on to his metallic digits.

While Krueger would, like most heels, reign supreme at the mic, we're just guessing physically he wouldn't be able to do much. Like Chucky, we think Freddy would make a far better manager. Seriously, someone call Chuck Palumbo.

Many opponents would kneel before General Zod. Far smarter than that idiot Non and far more attractive than the chick with a *Cagney & Lacey* haircut Ursa, Zod would dominate WWE TV with his great strength and smarts. We would like to see Zod's Flock in which he leads some other bad guys in sort of a Shield fashion. Or maybe we're misfiring here. Just throw an nWo sticker on his already black wardrobe and have him time travel to 1998 WCW television. It would be just too sweet!

Dr Evil wouldn't be a very formidable foe for anyone in the WWE Universe, that's for sure. Having said that the clueless wonder could become sort of a Million Dollar Man for this generation, offering rewards to top heels to take out top faces in the industry. Who are we kidding? The bounty he would offer probably wouldn't be reasonable enough for any bad guy to take on – well perhaps Virgil might.

Dr Evil would make for some good TV though. His promos would be priceless, and his secret weapon Mini Me could attack guys backstage – making us wonder, 'Can John Cena survive a heel bite from a Mini Heel?'

The Stay Puft Marshmallow Man would be way too big to fit inside any arena so he would have to be saved for outdoor WrestleMania or pay-per-view events or perhaps a match set in an open field somewhere. While he's cute and probably delicious, we think any of the big guys – be it a Big Show or Samoa Joe – would ultimately defeat the sugary monster by eating their way through his abdomen.

Since he's so bloated, we doubt Stay Puft would be able to manage any manoeuvre in the ring unless someone distracts his opponent in the ring, allowing him to stomp on them. That is why we suggest Jimmy Hart represents him, and he starts an immediate feud with John Cena. You can't see me? Hopefully.

Gollum is kind of a loser. He has no friends, he can't be trusted, and he is schizophrenic. He is also obsessed with a ring that holds amazing power. That is why we're betting if you were to throw him into a wrestling organisation, he would become obsessed with the championship belt.

But the deformed and cursed Hobbit wouldn't have a chance of fending off his opponents. He is not the strongest Hobbit ever (clearly Samwise holds that distinction), and is a bit of a wuss so we wouldn't expect him to intimidate anybody in the squared circle. But, he's one ugly MF and that needs to count for something.

So let's pair him with Predator and have them form a lethal tag team who would, at the very least, take home the tag titles. Predator can fight. Gollum can be sneaky. It is sort of an uglier, more intense version of the Kane/Daniel Bryan tandem. Zing.

Hannibal Lecter is a brilliant man – simply brilliant. He would outwit any opponent, and likely eat his way through to a number one contender spot. But, since WWE now forbids juicing and most controversial storylines, I find it highly doubtful Vince McMahon or Stephanie would give the thumbs up to a cannibalistic heel. Then again, Vince did come up with the Katie Vick storyline so anything is possible.

Jason Voorhees is probably not interested in taking on Kane. He seems to favour slaughtering hot teenagers at a summer camp, and we highly doubt he would find the time to enter a ring and clothesline anybody. But, since we're imagining a world where fictional bad guys become real life fake bad guys, we'll say Jason and his hockey mask gimmick could really take off.

Just create a back story that sometime between stints at Camp Crystal Lake, he trained at Stu Hart's dojo. Ask the big guy to leave his machete at home, and let his fists and headbutts do the talking. If he takes any advice, and you would never know because the dude doesn't talk much, we think he would become the top heel in the company. He has got the moves. He has got the looks. All he needs is Slick to manage him, and possibly Leatherface to join a potential stable, and we're all set.

Lex Luthor is a pretty cool villain in the comics, but Gene Hackman's cartoonish over-the-top portrayal in the original film series makes us think that incarnation would go over as well as a fart in a bucket. Have you tried that? Neither have we, but it would be pretty pointless. Hackman's Luthor sports wigs, and loves to cash in against Superman so we're betting he would make a good sidekick should Ted DiBiase Sr. make a comeback and drop Virgil like a bad habit. Don't count on it.

Magneto is a smart cookie who could easily win matches by outsmarting weaker opponents in the ring with his mind tricks. But, let's be honest. If he is going to go around and bend metal objects and make them move around, the wrestling ring is going to collapse and nobody wins. If Magneto can keep his powers in check, we think he can easily defeat a Kofi Kingston or Shelton Benjamin. If he doesn't, well, let's just hope WWE has a load of insurance.

Patrick Bateman would be a terrific heel manager. Sure, he's as fit as a fiddle, but he's so emotionally and mentally unstable that we think he would just burn out as a grappler. We suggest pitting the Wall Street suit with CM Punk, and let the two of them destroy opponents with their razor-sharp mic skills. Suggestion: lose 'Cult of Personality' and use a Huey Lewis song as an intro.

Norman Bates likes to wear dresses, and so did Adrian Adonis. Unfortunately for Norman, Adonis passed away decades ago, leaving quite a void in the flamboyant category of wrestling. If WWE could somehow bring back Billy and Chucky and turn them into Brokeback heels, we would pay to see Norman leading them to the ring in his terrible curly blonde wig. On second thought, start a story angle where Norman becomes infatuated with Linda McMahon and thinks she is his long-lost mum. She is not doing anything currently is she?

T-1000 has the ability to morph into anything and anyone and those traits would no doubt help him out in the ring. Assuming no babyface would have access to molten metal and a grenade, we think T-1000 could handily defeat a variety of opponents from high flyers like Evan Bourne to punch-and-kick all-stars like 'Taker (not at WrestleMania of course).

Since mic skills aren't exactly his strong suit ('Have you seen this boy' works in a movie – but not in a locker room), we would ask Ricardo Rodriguez to give this dude from Skynet a chance.

Jaws is a shark, and shouldn't be allowed to wrestle. For one thing, he doesn't have hands and kills people with his teeth. Secondly, he has less charisma than Snitsky and less mobility than an 85-year-old Freddie Blassie. But, we'll give him the benefit of the doubt, assume WWE forgoes its 'non-human ban' in the ring, and ban him from using his teeth in a match against a man with no teeth: Bushwhacker Luke. Good luck Luke. You will need it.

Let's be honest, the Wicked Witch of the West is a whiny bitch. She picks on teenage girls, and has some weird hatred for dogs. PETA would have been all on this had she entered WWE when it was WWF and pets ran supreme from Matilda to Damien. But let's not discredit the woman. She would make a ruthless diva and would certainly have more heat than Kong did. If approved to use her broom and flying monkeys there's no telling how far she could go. A dream meeting would be the WWOTW v Chyna in a bra and panties match.

George 'The Animal' Steele meant no harm to Miss Elizabeth. He just wanted her to be his friend – sort of like how Odie was to John or, to a lesser degree, Garfield. Bowser, on the other hand, wanted Princess Peach for all the wrong reasons, and since *Super Mario Bros.* was a kids' game, get your mind out of the gutter.

The villain, who also had the moniker King Koopa until Nintendo higher-ups dropped it because they realised it was a lame name, wanted to gain control of the princess's Mushroom Kingdom. For whatever reason, however, as evidenced by countless sequels he failed to do so.

But we applaud his perseverance and since Vince Jr has an affinity for big bad guys, we think he would fit right in with WWE. With a change of focus, this green monster, who has minions of ghosts and evil mushrooms who do his dirty work (not those mushrooms, stoner friends), could dominate with some killer moves. We already know he can jump higher than Earthquake could back in the day, but we also think a Bowser splash could be the biggest thing to happen to the top rope of wrestling since Randy Savage jumped off it.

We suggest Bowser take on another short Italian in Santino Marella, and see how it all shakes out. He can also see if Wario wants to help assist him outside the ring. After all, Bowser isn't as flexible as a Kardashian.

Bald Bull gets all the press, but King Hippo had it going on in Mike Tyson's Punch-Out. Drawn to perfection from Nintendo nerds, this villain looked like Viscera but with bigger man boobs. While he hit hard in the video game, a couple of blows to the stomach is all it took to knock the mammal down. The crowned hippo could fit right in during WWE's King of the Ring event as a man who already deems himself king and has nothing to prove to anybody. He would instantly get heel heat, and could establish himself as the most dangerous big man in the game right now.

That said, the character can't really be taken seriously. We haven't played the game in a while but the guy looks more like a toad, and we're pretty sure he farts during the game – or perhaps that's just our imagination. If he can work on guarding his gut a little, we would have him take on Goldust assuming that the 'Shattered Dreams' weirdo would return to the ring to fight a Brodus Clay clone with reptile features.

Ben Linus is a douche bag. On *Lost*, he conned a bunch of good guys, and killed the show's heart and soul in John Locke. But there's no mistaking it: he's a genius. Plus, he loves bunnies but that's neither here nor there. We would love to see the man also known as Henry Gale form a formidable stable called The Others or The Initiative and reign over wrestling like the nWo once did.

He could be sort of the Eric Bischoff to Hulk Hogan's nWo in that he could be an integral member of a group, but never gets his hands dirty. Or, he gets his hands dirty, but doesn't care. Some suggested wrestlers who would take flight with Linus calling the shots: Wade Barrett, Damien Sandow, R-Truth, and The Miz. Sorry Van Hammer…not you.

Mr Burns reigns over Springfield like a dark cloud that drizzles the weakest raindrop. In the wrestling ring this fruity suit would get eaten up like a Mars bar at a chocolate parade. That is why we would suggest Mr Burns stick with Smithers and never enter the ring. But if he ignored our advice, and suited up, Burns would become a jobber with a fat wallet – losing out on matches against everyone from Zack Ryder to even Michael Cole.

That is why we would put Mr Burns with Jack Swagger. There has never been a male manager who has the hots for his 'client' before, and it would make for a killer storyline. Sorry folks, Rico doesn't count. He could wrestle just as well as Billy or Chucky. Suggested intro music for Mr Burns: 'Disco Inferno'. Suggested finisher: running into the locker room on roller skates.

Jack Torrance was bat-shit crazy, but he would fit in so well with fellow supernaturalish star the Undertaker as a heel manager. Paul Bearer is gone, and may he rest in peace, so why not partner 'Taker with a lonely writer used to being stuck in a spooked hotel? Torrance could be that crazed, nutty valet the wrestling world needs, and could actually be the first wrestling personality to enter the ring with a typewriter. One would think I.R.S. might have, but even he knew his gimmick was cheesy enough without taking it to the ring.

Who shot J.R.? Who cares anymore? The Texas oil SOB could ride shotgun with JBL and dominate as ruthless businessmen who con their way to the top. If Donald Trump could get inducted in the WWE Hall of Fame, I see no reason why J.R. Ewing couldn't reign in the wrestling world. He is smart. He is rich, and he is far bitchier than Alexis Carrington ever was.

Dracula probably wouldn't go over very well in the wrestling world. As history has shown, Vampiro crapped the proverbial bed in wrestling and a vampire gimmick, while trendy, just wouldn't work well in this current wrestling climate. Should Dracula want to take a shot, we suggest he keep his mouth shut, fight, turn into a bat, and then fly around the ring to distract opponents. If he repeats this throughout a 15-minute cycle, we think he would do alright. First opponent? Have him wrestle Mae Young.

Voldemort probably can't blow his nose, but that has nothing to do with his wrestling career. The power-thirsty wizard has few redeeming qualities, killed a kid's parents, and wanted to kill Harry Potter himself, so he clearly has issues and questionable motives. But, his look is pretty lame and unattractive and we know where The Boogeyman ended up. A short wrestling shelf life would be the best Voldemort could expect. If he decides to lace up his boots, we suggest he take on the Great Muta in a battle of ugliness.

Catherine Tramell was a famous author who might have killed a lover of hers. She also swung both ways, and showed her Virginia to a bunch of cops. How that might translate in the wrestling world remains to be seen, but we would like to see how the ice-pick-wielding, sexy ice queen would do in the Divas division. Did we mention we saw the *Basic Instinct* character's Virginia?

10
Foreign Objects 101

OFTEN used to give the villain an unfair advantage, over the years the foreign object has become an institution among the wrestling world's rudest, crudest and most dastardly batch of goons. While a round trip ticket to Parts Unknown remains a mystery here is the closest you will ever come to a pair of brass knuckles without getting knocked out cold.

Asian green mist: Used to blind opponents, this mysterious green substance has been the go-to foreign object for many Asian superstars over the years. For decades this evil green liquid has spewed from stars such as the Great Kabuki and Killer Khan to most recently the Great Muta and Tajiri.

Guitar: The Honky Tonk Man was not only the greatest Intercontinental Champion of all time but he also introduced Greg 'The Hammer' Valentine to a bottle of jet-black hair dye among other things. However his most successful contribution to the ring and for the sake of this book was the 'prop' guitar.

Sure we cringe at the thought of the HTM defeating Ricky Steamboat, but it was music to our ears whenever he smashed his favourite tune on an opponent's head. During WCW's closing act Jeff Jarrett brought guitar wielding back to the spotlight and was swinging for the Monday night fences in all his 'Slapnut' t-shirt glory.

Sledgehammer: Not just an over-played Peter Gabriel video from the 1980s. The sledgehammer has been a part of the Triple H repertoire for some time now. Not quite as merchandisable as 'Hacksaw' Jim Duggan's 'Hoooo' wood, but this particular choice of weaponry has helped make HHH both a household name and a top heel for many years.

Cheese grater: Usually reserved for Sunday afternoon brunch at Grandma Miele's, the cheese grater found new purpose in the form of Extreme Championship Wrestling's hardcore lifestyle. Rather than using the kitchen utensil for its sole purpose of grating all things mozzarella, Tommy Dreamer and company altered the course of wrestling history forever and soon thereafter grating foreheads was as common a sight as a clothesline or a drop toehold.

Shock stick: The Fabulous Rougeau Brothers dabbled in tag team mediocrity for years until Ray was forced to retire, thus thrusting younger brother Jacques Rougeau into the role of Royal Canadian Mounted Policeman turned wrestling rule-breaker where he even captured an Intercontinental Championship win over Bret Hart.

With help from his trusty cattle prod the obnoxious Canadian feuded with a who's who of WWE faces including Big Bossman, Tito Santana and Roddy Piper. Despite making Jacques relevant the shock stick's greatest victory was teaming with Kevin Nash to dethrone the undefeated Goldberg streak in one of WCW's darkest hours.

Salt: Now used solely to add much needed flavour to a bland potato chip and/or French fry, salt was once regarded as one of the premier foreign objects for a wrestling villain to rely on. Of course the most famous salt tossing sighting was at WrestleMania IX when Bret Hart fell victim to the treacherous trajectory of Mr Fuji's blinding salt thus paving the way for Yokozuna's 60-second reign as WWE Champion.

Tennis racket: If we had a dollar for every match that the Midnight Express won due to the aid of Jim Cornette's better half there is no doubt we would be filthy rich. That being said, the tennis racket played an influential role in the careers of Cornette-managed teams throughout the 1980s. It could even be said that wrestling's most controversial accessories helped usher in the likes of the Jimmy Hart megaphone and Paul E. Dangerously's larger-than-life-itself cellphone.

Black forearm band: Hands down the most pointless foreign object in history – besides Lex Luger's loaded bionic forearm – was the black armband worn by perennial jobber Iron Mike Sharpe. About as pointless as a Koko B. Ware music video for the *Piledriver* album, Sharpe hardly ever won a match with his gimmicky extra let alone get his own LJN wrestling figure and even Ted Arcidi scored one of those bad boys.

Steel chair: Take it from us, you cannot write an accurate tale of debauchery and pro wrestling tomfoolery without mention of the infamous steel chair. Winning more matches than even a Hogan leg drop, the chair itself has probably screwed over more good guys than Mr McMahon. About as basic as John Cena's 'five moves of doom', the chair has one simple approach to reach absolute success – simply swing for the fences and all your dastardly dreams will be answered.

11
How To Be A Heel – Twenty Badass Steps At Being A Badass

1 – Cutting a promo: One of the key proponents for any wrestling personality good or bad. In other words in order to get over with the crowd your mic skills have got to be at the top of their game. Despite other means at filling this need existing (see #7 or #18) if you are lacking in this department you may want to choose a new profession.

2 – Grab the tights: Not to be confused with the Junkyard Dog's catchy *Wrestling Album* riff 'Grab Them Cakes'. If it's instant heel heat you so desire then your best option en route to going full-on baddie is by grabbing a fistful of spandex on your way to yet another controversial three-count.

3 – Eye gouge: Don't let that chiselled physique and fake spray-on tan fool you. One quick thumb to the eye socket and that goody two shoes will go down faster than you can say Sir Oliver Humperdink.

4 – Remove the turnbuckle: When a steel chair is not an option your plan B should always be the exposed turnbuckle. Granted you're not going to go full-on George Steele on the sucker, but just quickly remove the padding and you're off to breaking every ring rule in no time.

5 – Support foreign soil: As 'U-S-A! U-S-A!' chants blare through arenas across the country it's your job to frown upon the stars and stripes and remain loyal to your non red white and blue allegiance. You are an easy mark for a cup of beer to the head so don't say we did not warn you.

6 – Interference: Ninety per cent of your matches must end with some outside distraction so pick your poison and make sure you have a sinister sidekick who is certain to be up to the daily task of doing your dirty work.

7 – Hire a manager: If you're not pushing your weight in hate or your spoken word is not up to par this may be your best bet at garnering legitimate hatred from the loyal wrestling fan base. A manager or advisor (whatever it is they call them these days) is not just your scrawny accessory but the sinister mastermind can also double as your cock-of-the-walk mouthpiece.

8 – Utilise the double team: For all you tag team specialists out there make sure you cut the ring in half and master the art of the blind tag for good measure. Of course it always helps when the guy in the zebra stripes is oblivious to all of your treacherous tag tricks.

9 – The low blow: The most blatant of all manoeuvres, the nut shot is a sure-fire way to earning a one-way ticket to the heel locker room.

Coming in all shapes, sizes and directions for that matter the junk punch is your one-stop shop for your entire rule-breaking needs. Sure the kick is one way to go but we prefer the obnoxiously thrown uppercut to the man parts.

10 – Taunting: This 'kicking him while he's down' mantra has always been a vital lesson learned in rule-breaking 101. Sure, it will garner a 15-yard penalty in football, but in this game belittling your opponent with some potent vocab will make you a top heel in no time.

11 – Use the ropes to your advantage: A tainted three-count is not a tainted three-count without the assistance of the ringside ropes. When your opponent is down and out just add insult to injury and place those size 11s on the middle rope for some much-needed leverage.

12 – Work the five-count: Not to be confused with the Bundy five-count, this diabolical manoeuvre is best practised either by milking a choke hold or by shoving an opponent's neck between the ropes before the referee can get to five.

13 – Insult the fans: The cheapest of all cheap heat; just grab a mic and start throwing some trusty hate bombs on the people that spend their hard-earned dollar to see you get your tail kicked. Entertainment at its finest.

14 – Turn on your bestie: You can conquer death rumours and resurface in a bowling alley but your claim to fame will be turning your back on your best bud and joining the dark side.

15 – Spit: Often running hand in hand with a slap to the face, spitting may not pack the same punch but it certainly propels any feud lacking in controversy and it is sure to help build up to a gimmick match or three.

16 – Use an object: You can easily go the roll of nickels route on this one or perhaps a pair of brass knuckles is your calling, but either way if you're going to be an evil-doer you might as well do it right. These days to make an impact the Singapore cane or the trash can lid make the most noise but why not keep it simple and get right to the point? On that note can someone please pass a fork.

17 – Change the hardware: An extreme makeover would be to toss your newly won hardware in the trash to make an immediate statement and ignite an extreme revolution in the process. If that's not your cup of tea then try spray-painting your team colours on the game's most coveted jewel.

18 – Valet: Every bad guy needs some scantily-clad eye-candy as well as a ratings-maker to cower behind when the crap hits the fan. Your ascension to fame and heel fortune just very well may depend on the hottie in high heels doing your dirty work.

19 – Get yourself disqualified/counted out: When the going gets tough the tough get in the ring to finish the fight. But in the case of our cowardly heel it's best to hit the high road with your tail tucked between your hot pink tights and get the heck out of dodge.

20 – Grow a beard: Nothing says anti-establishment more than a little five o'clock shadow. As the booing intensifies so does the facial stubble and alas career-altering changes are in full swing and another 'bad guy beard' is born.

12
Movies Gone Bad

WHETHER it's *No Holds Barred* or *The Chaperone*, WWE has been responsible for more bad films than Charlie Sheen or Shannon Tweed ever made. In our parallel universe of a book, here's a list of five films we're thankful never happened.

Three Heels and a Baby: Jake Roberts, King Kong Bundy, and the Honky Tonk Man star as themselves in a story that centres on them being left alone with a baby at an arena. Hi-jinx and terrible plotlines ensue in this would-be comedy.

Piledriver – The Movie: Will the nWo prevent Koko B. Ware from dancing with a hard hat on his head and a bird on his shoulder at a construction site? Find out this and more in this Ivan Reitman-produced comedy about single guys looking for love on their lunch hour.

Country Boy – The Hillbilly Jim Story: Zach Galifinakis stars as the wrestling 'legend' in this fictionalised story about a man who went from working on a farm to working out in a ring. Look for a cameo from Ned Beatty as Uncle Elmer.

The Village Idiot: M. Night Shyamalan's unexpected sequel to 2003's *The Village* stars the WWE Universe's Eugene as a mysterious man who befriends the townfolk in the isolated town from the first one. Bryce Dallas Howard reprises her role and Jim 'The Anvil' Neidhart appears as a gas station owner with an axe to grind.

Suburban Nanny: In a dual role, Hulk Hogan portrays his characters from *Mr Nanny* and *Suburban Commando* as long-lost twins who try to stop a villainous oil company CEO played by Gene Snitsky from drilling in his family's backyard.

13
Heel Turns On The Fans

LIKE most professional sports teams (unless you're the New York Yankees who buy their way to the play-offs each year), professional wrestling comes in hot and cold streaks. When things are going good, it's going really good. And when it's bad? Boy, is it New York Mets bad.

There are plenty of books where you can read about the highest highs and the lowest lows in the squared circle, but not like this. Below are moments in which wrestling writers, executives, and even toy makers pulled heel turns on a loyal fan base. These are great moments in terrible cheap heat, personality disorders, poorly-constructed storylines, and everything inbetween.

A day that will live in infamy
On 23 March 2001, Vince McMahon's WWE purchased its chief competitor WCW, and put the final nail

in the coffin for the mid-to-late 1990s 'golden years' of wrestling. Without competition, the product went the way of a Last Dragon screening at the Alamo.

Blame Canada
In 2001, as WCW clung to life like a Brooke Shields sitcom, the writers turned to cheap heat by having American 'hero' 'Hacksaw' Jim Duggan shave his beard and join Lance Storm's Team Canada. We didn't like it the first time when it was Sgt. Slaughter becoming an Iraqi sympathiser at the height of the Gulf War and we didn't like it then. Seeing a beardless Duggan in a Sue Sylvester jumpsuit and Canadian flag felt as normal as a dolphin on an exercise bike.

July 1987
Much like the sno-cone and the ice cream sandwich, two staples within the ice cream truck community, it did not take long for the WWE Superstars Ice Cream Bars to become a favourite among kids of all shapes and sizes. Much tastier than a Hulk Hogan protein shake, the creamy vanilla ice cream bar, complete with chocolate coating on the back topped with a giant cookie imprinted with your favourite WWE superstar, was a huge hit in frozen food aisles across the nation. The ice cream bar remains one of the most sought-after wrestling items still talked about today and just as elusive as snatching a George 'The Animal' Steele Mine Doll on eBay. Please Vince, stop the hate and bring back the cookie.

December 1987
For years the heel has taken short cuts, rule-breaking and foreign object use to new heights but to this day no wrestling antagonist has ever stooped as low as the 'Million Dollar Man' Ted DiBiase as he embarked his pretentious persona on to the grand stage of WWE. Whether he was kicking newlyweds out of their honeymoon suite or paying Andre the Giant to hand over the WWE Championship nothing can compare to the dastardly act of kicking the ball away at the 14th dribble after he bet a kid from the audience $100 that he could not bounce a basketball 15 times.

One Man Gang was Akeem
Yeah, we know One Man Gang was re-packaged as Akeem back in the day. We didn't accept it, but we applauded the audacity of the writers to create such a stereotypically bad gimmick. But, in 1994, when a similar big bad guy got repackaged as The Shark, we winced more than a whiff of Justin Bieber's latest fragrance. Earthquake was and will always be Earthquake. Sorry WCW, we just didn't buy the big guy in a cheap mask that we wouldn't let our three-year old wear at Halloween. And Tiny Lister, consider yourself lucky that we're not name-dropping Z-Gangsta here.

What a rush?
On 28 July 2005, John Heidenreich started tag-teaming with Animal and they became the Road Warriors 2.0. Heidenreich never could replace the dearly-departed

Hawk, but it's not his fault. The writers should have realised he would go over like a fart in a crowded baby pool.

Oh no…LJN

Andre the Giant was literally the biggest star in WWE. He warranted an action figure that resonated with fans who wanted to play with his likeness at home. Instead, LJN created a rubbery figure that could best be described as Roseanne Barr's head on a sumo wrestler's body. Thankfully, years later, they introduced a new figure with shorter hair that – at the very least – resembled a man.

New Blood

Several babyfaces make the transition to heel quite easily. Hulk Hogan did it at Bash at the Beach. Rick Martel did it. Paul Orndorff did as well. Other grapplers, however, have a harder time. Take Goldberg for example, who decided to align himself with Vince Russo and become a member of the New Blood back in 2000. The heel turn was as short-lived as one of his movies in the cinemas.

Goose egg

On 22 November 1990, Gobbledy Gooker made its debut at a sold-out Survivor Series. On paper, it shouldn't have worked: a wrestler – in this case Hector Guerrero – decked out as a giant, wrestling bird. In reality, it didn't work. What a bold, terrible move.

What came first? The chicken? The egg? Certainly not the ratings.

Powerless
In 1993, Paul Roma, one half of the tag turd Power and Glory, was appointed to arguably the biggest stable in wrestling history: the Four Horsemen. Put your thumb, index finger, pinky, and fourth finger down, and stick the other one up. That represents what was done to the fans.

And new heavyweight champion…that annoying guy from *Scream*
The nails were being hammered into the coffin for months, but perhaps the final one – not counting Vince Jr.'s acquisition of the company – was when WCW put the World Heavyweight Championship belt around actor David Arquette's waist following a tag match with him and Diamond Dallas Page against Eric Bischoff and Jeff Jarrett.

Sadly, it may have been more entertaining than *Scream 3*.

Pay-per-screw
Back in the day, we enjoyed the build-up for WrestleMania. Eventually, we would be excited for Survivor Series, and then SummerSlam, and the Royal Rumble. There were four big wrestling events each year, and that was enough. Then, the 1990s came and they become monthly affairs that just continue to rise

for fans financially. Vince screwed Bret? More like Vince screwed us.

Kane bangs dead chicks?
In October 2002, WWE started arguable its worst gimmick ever. OK, it's not arguable. It is, was, and will be the worst ever. HHH teased he knew a secret about Kane, and eventually revealed that the Big Red Machine was a murderer. The story went that Kane used to date a chick named Katie Vick, and he killed her in a drunk-driving accident. HHH mocked him for weeks – imitating him at a fake funeral for the fake dead girl. We will stop right there. It sucked, and lingered like a bad fart for way too many weeks.

14
Dream Matches

NOT to be confused with the New World Order's bad-guy-themed pay-per-view called Souled Out, we decided to match up some of the very best in the biz with, well, some of the very best in the biz.

Opening match:

John Cena v an oven mitt

It is our dream card and if we are calling the shots we are going to have the most over-rated WWE Champion wrestle on the pre-show against an oven mitt. Our guess is you bought this book because you root for the bad guy and certainly not because you are knee-deep in Fruity Pebbles and Cenation wristbands. OK, maybe we are a bit harsh, but wouldn't it be a Kodak moment watching the Doctor of Thuganomics drop his five-knuckle shuffle on the world's most talked-about cooking accessory? Honestly it can't be much worse than when Davey Boy Smith was back dropped by The Rock on a pile of dog shit during an episode of *Raw*.

The crowd-stealer:

Mr Perfect v Chris Jericho

Forget the match, which would probably outshine any and all main events on the card, the most anticipated battle between the game's greatest Intercontinental Champions (sorry Honky Tonk) would be the highly entertaining pre-match banter. Sure Hennig can bowl with the best of them and he even beat Nick Bockwinkel when the AWA was still relevant but Y2J was and is the first ever undisputed champion and for that the slight edge goes to the Fozzy front man, of course no offence to the West Texas Rednecks.

The instant classic:

Randy Savage v Shawn Michaels

Years before the Heartbreak Kid was gloating about his main event status and headlining on the grandest of stages it was the Macho Man who was stealing the show and making 'Mania moments of his very own. This one is a toss-up – do you go with the once-proud king of wrestling not named Haku or do you put your money on the guy who still claims to be the 'main event' even though his best days are behind him and only makes random appearances dressed like he belongs on reality television's *Duck Hunters*? The match would be a true classic for sure, a 35–40-minute masterpiece, but when the dust clears do you go with the Mega Power or the Rocker? Exactly.

The streak continues:

Undertaker v the Great Muta

Sure, this one will probably not put butts in the 'Mania seats, but let's face it some of Undertaker's past victims have not or will not ever be the cream of the wrestling crop (take that Mr Nathan Jones). That being said this is a compelling match that is sure to leave wrestling purists moist in the spandex. Muta's international appeal and in-ring work have left their mark on the business for over two decades and of course the Deadman's résumé speaks for itself. If this match happens in the 1990s it's a dream match for the ages and if it happens today it's most likely a mid-card classic. Oh who are we kidding, we would still watch. Our pick is the Undertaker with or without his lame biker gimmick.

The main event:

Bret Hart v Kurt Angle v CM Punk

Not a mark for the triple threat but this match would almost certainly be a game-changer. Imagine all three of these guys in their prime and in the ring and you've got a unanimous match of the year winner. In one corner you've got the Excellence of Execution, the Best in the World in another and the only Olympic gold medal winner in pro wrestling ready to suplex anyone who gets in his bald-headed way. Nobody loses in this three-way for the ages. In fact the only winners would be the fans grateful enough to be witness to history.

15
What Heel Would You Want In Your Corner During a Zombie Apocalypse?

ANDRE the Giant is big, but he is slower than a fat kid running track in middle school with Abe Vigoda strapped to his back. Jake 'The Snake' Roberts has quick wit, and could likely use Damien as bait for one or two walkers, but chances are slim he would be able to talk himself out of becoming lunch. Here are a few heels who would give you a fighting chance against the undead:

Rick Rude: In his heyday, the 'Ravishing' one made it with the ladies, and made faces look bad in the ring. He had a hell of a work ethic, and one hot bod. That is why we would pick him to help us out of an alleyway filled with zombies. With that body, he could likely outrun anybody, fight his way through crowds, and last all night long. That is what she said.

Ric Flair: To be the man you have to beat the man, at least that was the Nature Boy's motto during his 30-year-plus run as one of the villains in the industry. But let's be honest, even 'Slick' Ric would know to trade in those Rolex watches and custom suits, jump into that stretch limousine and plough right into those zombies. Marathon matches are gone and you sure as hell better hope the Horsemen got your back otherwise space mountain will be officially closed for business.

Mad Dog Vachon: Our guess would be that you want this guy on your side during any and all conflicts so why would that change when you are surrounded by a pack of walkers? An in-his-AWA-prime Vachon would almost certainly have put up a valiant fight and even a past-his-prime Mad Dog would have gone out swinging, prosthetic leg and all.

Baron von Raschke: This guy got more heat than just about anybody during his heyday as a rule-breaker. Research has shown that a sudden strike to the cranium is going to stop a zombie dead in its tracks. Would the Hall of Famer be able to claw his way out of a slew of blood-thirsty zombies? Not even Fritz Von Erich's handgrip is that bionic.

16
Heel Of The Moment – 100 Bad Guys Who Did A Whole Lot Of Good

BARNIE Fife might be your favourite sidekick of all time, but ours is Skippy from *Family Ties*. He never did get Mallory, but he always kept it real and stayed positive. Similarly, if we were to ask you – and by you we mean the individual reader (although it would be cool if thousands of people reading this collectively just shouted out their answer) – what your favourite album was, you might say *Dark Side of the Moon*.

Paul's Boutique from the Beastie Boys would be among our tops of all time. But, it's subjective. You know it. We know it. Even Eugene from the WWE Universe knows it. Anytime you put a 'best of' list together, people will wince with disgust or give you a figurative thumbs up.

The same is true in this passage of our book. You cannot write a heel-related book in wrestling without mentioning the tops of their trade. Below is our list of top 100 heels – in no particular order.

Again, what we might find the top of all time may not gel with you. Heck, you might even pull your own heel turn on us, and slam this book down. We respect that, and besides, it's not like Zeus cracks the top 100. There is no reason to get that upset. Anyway, here they are – our top baddies who took wrestling to new heights.

'Rowdy' Roddy Piper: A true original, which is saying a lot in wrestling, this wise-ass grappler could do it all. He could compete in the main event one night, host a hit show the next (Piper's Pit), or sometimes, actually do both. So many of the top 1980s moments feature Piper prominently whether it was cracking a coconut over Jimmy 'Superfly' Snuka's head or leading arguably the best interview segment of all time when Andre the Giant turned his back on Hulk Hogan – paving the way for a WrestleMania III epic match. We could go on and on, but we won't. Let's just say when it comes to heels, they don't get much better than the man in the kilt.

Earthquake: John Tenta once thrust his large body on a snake in a bag – in TV wonderland anyway. Yes, the big man was surprisingly agile for a man his size, and was pretty ruthless. He was a solid main-to-mid-carder and won the tag team belts with fellow weather-related gimmick Typhoon. Looking back, Tsunami might have been a better name, but Earthquake was a one-man wrecking crew, and we felt his aftershocks for many years. Damien did, as well. Google it. It was crazy.

Mr Perfect: If the teen nerds from the movie *Weird Science* perfected heel wrestlers from their computer much like they did a hottie like Kelly LeBrock, they would probably build Curt Hennig, AKA Mr Perfect. With an impressive physique, in-ring work ethic, and mic skills to boot, Hennig perfected the art of the heel. The son of Larry 'The Axe' Hennig made a name for himself quickly in the business, and especially in WWE. He had great runs with Bobby 'The Brain' Heenan and remains one of the top heels to ever grace the squared circle. One thing is for sure, no other grappler could have bragged about helping Wade 'Chicken Man' Boggs 'perfect' his swing.

Andre the Giant: 'Larger than life' is a term that gets used and abused more than Lindsay Lohan, but it works to great effect when referring to Andre Rousimoff. The WWE Hall of Famer and groundbreaking wrestler battled all of the greats from his era, and became a go-to good guy for years until he turned on Hulk Hogan and aligned himself with Bobby Heenan. The 1980s can arguably be defined by the 'Who Shot J.R.?' cliffhanger from *Dallas*, but for our money, we still remember where we were, who we were with, and what we were wearing (PJs of course) when Andre the Giant tore the Hulkster's cross from around his neck. This epic storyline delivered on every level leading up to the two icons' match at 'Mania, and Andre the Giant was arguably the biggest reason. If he couldn't sell being a heel he might have gone the way of Jimmy Snuka following his bout with Bob Backlund at The Garden. Obey indeed.

Bad News Brown: Jules from *Pulp Fiction* had a Bad Mother Fucker wallet, and he earned it. Well, in the wrestling world, Bad News Brown earned that moniker. A skilled wrestler who looked and talked like he was out of a Quentin Tarantino movie, Allen James Coage was a top heel for a few years with his no-nonsense style. The former Olympic judo master battled with many greats during his tenure at WWE from Randy Savage to Hulk Hogan, but our favourite heel turn was when he attacked president Jack Tunney on the Brother Love Show. Tunney was the company's fake president. Bad News Brown was its very real badass.

Slick: Ken Johnson is a lucky man. His 'performance' as WWE manager Slick could have set African Americans back a few decades. Instead, his fast-talking, Malcolm X-era-pimp-dressed, 'Jive Soul Bro' rapping schtick stuck with fans because he was so good at playing it so stereotypically bad. Sure, his clients weren't as big as other managers of that time like Jimmy Hart, but the Slickster managed former Blassie protégés Nikolai Volkoff and the Iron Sheik, Rick Martel, and Butch Reed for starters. We will throw him a mulligan for the Bolsheviks and Power and Glory because he managed to make the Twin Towers tandem of Akeem (AKA One Man Gang) and the Big Bossman relevant. Watch clips on YouTube, and you'll be stunned Akeem, in particular, rose to such heights! We think it was because Slick was in his corner. Like a pimple in the centre of your girlfriend's nose, you couldn't look away from Slick when he was at ringside or on camera. Added bonus: the 'reverend' once went bowling on camera with Kamala.

Big John Studd: Declaring yourself the 'true giant of wrestling' is a very tall order. That being said, Big John Studd has had to stare up at only a few men. Wrestling in the shadow of Hogan and Andre, Studd in all his star-studded tights glory held his own during WWE's foray into the pop culture landscape. As part of the Heenan Family he even managed to give Andre the Giant his first and only televised haircut. Of course it helped that Heenan crony Ken Patera backed the bearded baddie while all the Giant could muster was an S.D. Jones partnership.

However for all his heel treachery perhaps the highlight of his wrestling existence was being on the losing end of the inaugural WrestleMania's $15,000 Bodyslam Challenge. As Liberace was high stepping his way to Garden greatness with the Rockettes it was

Studd who was left flat on his back with $15,000 less in his wallet.

But it wasn't all sour grapes for Bobby Heenan's biggest asset as if not for Studd, who else would have feuded with the Machines? Speaking of masked men one thing we do know about Studd is the only WWE gold he held was ironically under a mask as part of the Executioners with his mentor Killer Kowalski.

Finally in an unrelated note *My Giant* starring Gheorghe Muresan and Billy Crystal was not based on his Hall of Fame career.

Raven: When Scott Levy made his way into the mainstream of World Championship Wrestling as surfboard-toting light heavyweight mid-carder Scotty Flamingo, the industry had no idea that the former manager of WWE tag champions the Quebecers (yes, we are talking about you Johnny Polo) would transform himself into a grunge-wearing sociopath known as Raven. A fixture in the land of Extreme Championship Wrestling and the poster boy for hardcore wrestling, the two-time ECW Champion has been a thorn in many a wrestler's side for years and years. Whether he was 'brainwashing' children or one-upping his summer camp nemesis Tommy Dreamer, Raven was and still is as bad as they come. With a Singapore cane in tow and an evenflow DDT waiting to be had this 27-time WWE Hardcore Champion (take that Yankees) continues to be a force in the independent scene. Known for his 'gimmick matches' and love for comic books, the rule-breaking Raven even went as far as to destroy Perry Saturn's one-time love interest Moppy the Mop.

Fabulous Moolah: All we can remember as fans of 1980s women's wrestling was that the Fabulous Moolah held the WWE Championship for 28 years before dropping the belt to Cyndi Lauper's protégé. Moolah was as tough as they came and while she may have jobbed to Wendi Richter in front of a live television audience that was perhaps more moist waiting for the next Divo or Eurythmics video, she got our revenge in the form of WWE's original pre-Montreal screwjob when she unmasked as the Spider Lady before a stunned MSG audience that saw her steal one away from the disgruntled Richter.

How many people, man or woman, can lay claim to being a world champion at the age of 76? In 1999 the incomparable Moolah did just that when she defeated Ivory for the strap. Sure you would have never seen the Fabulous one in a bra and panties dance-off that most current Divas flaunt around in these days but ask anybody and they will tell you that the Fabulous Moolah was as tough as they come – just don't tell Mae Young, who got powerbombed through a Dudley table not once but twice.

Chris Jericho: Whether he is headlining Wrestle-Mania or fronting his very own rock band Chris Jericho is not afraid to prove how great he truly is. In fact the Ayatollah of Rock 'n' Rolla has been making headlines and winning championships all over the world. A product of the Hart Dungeon (seriously, which Canadian wrestler hasn't been stretched in Stu's basement?), the man who introduced us to the Jeritron 6000 and Ralphus – his personal security from his days in WCW – has stolen the show in almost every promotion he has been a part of.

His debut in WWE still remains as one of the most anticipated and coolest debuts e-e-e-ever and on a side note it did not require gas masks and bottled water (take that Y2K). The former Lion Tamer and Highlight Reel host became the first ever undisputed champion of the world when he defeated Steve Austin and The Rock in one night and he has captured more Intercontinental Championships than any other wrestler in WWE history which includes his very first over Chyna.

Jerry 'The King' Lawler: Wrestling has had its fair share of royalty. Over the years the crown has helped the careers of many a man. It made Haku relevant (although we would never say that to his face because he would probably kick our butts) and the Macho King was so hated that he even got Sapphire over with the fans. Even Booker T dabbled in royalty at one point (can you say better career move than G.I. Bro) and Harley Race even went the king route and got coroneted for the sake of making a quick buck and joining the WWE gimmick circus.

However no King has garnered more heat than one Jerry 'The King' Lawler. These days he still cracks jokes and delivers one-liners like no other as he co-pilots *Raw* but back in his heyday he was hell bent on making life miserable for the likes of Bret Hart, 'Rowdy' Roddy Piper and even you Doink and Dink. Sure he is a grown man walking around with a crown but nobody – and we mean nobody – can deliver a piledriver quite like the King.

Jesse Ventura: His brightest days in the ring were as part of the East/West Connection with Adrian Adonis but in fact 'The Body' is best known for his heel commentary during WWE programming throughout the 1980s. Being partial to villains was his calling card and for the first six 'Manias and most *Saturday Night's Main Event* specials Ventura was in your living room setting the stage for yet another exciting night of pro wrestling. After a spat with WWE boss Vince McMahon the future Governor of Minnesota eventually took his talents to Superbrawl and joined forces with World Championship Wrestling. While he talked a great game for the sake of entertainment Ventura soon looked to other outlets such as Hollywood to show off his amazing talents. He has performed in *Predator*, *Demolition Man* and of course *The Running Man* in which he played a character called Captain Freedom. He is an innovator in terms of building the mould for the quintessential heel commentator and who knows, maybe one day we will see a wrestler in the White House.

The Iron Sheik: One thing we regret not seeing during the days when George Steele was tearing up turnbuckles is that the Jumping Bomb Angels never made it to LJN wrestling doll status. Talk about your heel turns. OK, so did we get your attention? Speaking of heels did the Iron Sheik ever get his rematch after Hogan broke out of the camel clutch and started an American pop culture phenomenon? Sure, the guy is whacked out of his mind and he will be remembered more for his *Stern Show* exploits than his wrestling accolades but back in the day the Iranian mad man could compete with the very best of them. He terrorised good guys for decades, he has got the coolest wrestling boots in history and his moustache – well maybe you should have read our first book. Led by 'Classy' Freddie Blassie, a badass dude in his own right, the native of Tehran in Iran is the most recognised transition champion in wrestling history. That being said someone call up Vince because WrestleMania XXX is around the corner so let's give the Sheik that re-match he deserves and who knows, maybe almost some 40 years later the Hulkster will be less likely to kick out of that dreaded clutch.

Christian: Sodas rule. This wreaks of awesomeness. Yep, Christian was one half of an often hilarious tandem with Edge, but he also played the role of individual competitor pretty damn well too. Whether in TNA Impact Wrestling or going it alone or with fellow funny smartass Chris Jericho, Christian matched his in-ring flair with mic skills that a guy like Bobby Lashley would kill for. A versatile competitor who always put his body in danger with his various TLC matches and ladder matches, Christian has always been a solid upper middle-carder with flashes of main-event status. In 2011, he won the World Heavyweight Championship following former partner Edge's retirement, but he lost it two days later. He deserved better, and hopefully 'Captain Charisma' will get another run with the gold one day. Sodas, by the way, do rule. Just don't tell former New York Mayor Mike Bloomberg to super-size it.

Daniel Bryan: Easily the most exciting wrestler working today, the man born Bryan Danielson has got it all: the look, the attitude, the mic skills, and most of all the ring skills to become one of the greatest stars this industry has ever seen. With a beard that looks more suited for Jim Breuer's *Saturday Night Live* Goat Boy and a tagline that sways from 'Yes! Yes! Yes' to 'No! No! No!' the always amusing Bryan has become a force to be reckoned with in WWE. With solid moves – his dragon suplex is flawless and his cobra clutch would make Sgt. Slaughter cry – it's no wonder WWE continually pushes this pint-sized juggernaut. From his battles with The Miz to his oddball partnership with Kane, we're always saying 'Yes' to this often self-deprecating heel.

Big Show: Whether he was the nWo's Giant or WWE's Big Show, Paul Wight can get around pretty damn well for a man billed as seven feet tall and over 400 pounds. With a devastating finisher (the chokeslam), and a painfully obvious theme song to enter the ring with, Big Show is arguably one of the top ten heels in the business currently working today. Well, OK probably by the time you read this he'll switch over to being a face. Big Show, for us anyway, seems to switch between heel and face more than Sarah Jessica Parker changed her dresses on *Sex and the City*. That said, let's focus on how bad Show has been. Wight was discovered by Hulk Hogan, who brought him into WCW, but he earned his stripes fairly quickly – winning the WCW World Heavyweight Championship and becoming a mainstay in its programming until he jumped ship to WWE in 1999. Throughout his lengthy run with the McMahon company Show has feuded with just about every big name in the business, from John Cena to Brock Lesnar to Hulk Hogan. Heck, he even wrestled a sumo wrestler at a WrestleMania and an utterly useless Mark Henry for a while. Show makes a solid face, but we're happier when he takes an about face and portrays the big, bad pain-in-the-ass heel that he was born to be. Who cares if he's not really Andre the Giant's son.

Big Bossman: For a man who sadly died at just 41, Ray Traylor had legs in the wrestling business. The man who wrestled as Jim Cornette's muscle Bubba Rogers in the UWF and Big Bossman in the WWE had a fruitful near-20-year career in WWE and WCW, and battled the likes of Hulk Hogan, Rick Rude and 'Macho

Man' Randy Savage. On paper, Big Bossman probably shouldn't have worked as well as it did but Traylor sold the gimmick well and really made us believe he was a prison guard. Obviously, he wasn't. Just like Akeem wasn't um, a guy named Akeem.

Chris Benoit: Trained by Stu Hart and the Hart brothers, there was arguably never a better in-ring performer than Chris Benoit. We all know the story by now – how in June 2007 he murdered his wife and young son (and then killed himself) – but if we could just focus on the wrestling for a minute (we know it's nearly impossible), the Crippler was one of the best the business ever saw. When he was a heel, you hated him. When he was a face, you cheered him on as if you were in the ring. Physically and technically, he was just the best, and it's devastating that he tarnished his legacy and took the lives of two innocent souls.

Bam Bam Bigelow: Those tattoos on his head looked so damn cool, but they must have hurt like a son-of-a-bitch. Scott Bigelow, AKA Bam Bam Bigelow, made his impact known in the wrestling world almost immediately. The Beast From The East looked intimidating with his big physique, sinister look, and tattooed noggin but he actually pulled off being a face for quite a while. But, we'll remember him more for playing it bad – from his WrestleMania XI match against former linebacker Lawrence Taylor to his feuds with Hulk Hogan and Bret Hart to name two – this surprisingly agile in-ring performer was one of the top heels in the pre-Attitude Era and helped shape ECW into the cult force it became with his iconic matches against the likes of Shane Douglas, Taz, and Rob Van Dam. Off camera, he was supposedly a sweetheart who actually risked his life to save children in a fire in 2000. The man who 'greeted' opponents with his Asbury Park finisher died at just 45 years old in 2007 – cheating fans out of many more memorable matches from the Jersey-bred grappler.

Big Van Vader: Before spanning the world as a bona fide superstar the man known as Vader was dabbling in Minnesota as AWA mid-carder Leon 'Baby Bull' White. Soon however Vader was unleashed to the masses and with his cruiserweight-like agility in a super heavyweight-type body the masked behemoth was destined to take over the world. His path of destruction led him to three WCW Championships and the right ear of Cactus Jack, which was lost in a violent match in Germany. Although he never captured the brass ring in WWE it was always Vader time-time-time whenever the beast wanted to moonsault an opponent or drop a Vader bomb or three.

Bruiser Brody: If you're going to get into a legitimate brawl you had better make sure that Bruiser Brody has got your back. The unpredictable Brody beat to his own drum while freelancing around the wrestling world and he is considered to be one of the most dangerous big men of all time. He sometimes refused to job to other stars and his uncooperative behaviour at times made him a must-see personality. His greatest success was overseas in Japan and in Puerto Rico where he had bloody feuds with Abdullah the Butcher and island fixture Carlos Colon.

Harley Race: Always ready for a fight, 'Handsome' Harley Race was as rugged and tough as they come. The eight-time (when the belt wasn't changed as often as a pair of underpants) NWA Champion defended his title all throughout the territories and against all comers. It is safe to say he was a fighting champion and if he could wrestle eight nights a week he probably would. He had a Hall of Fame career and it is hard to argue that Race is not among the top ten technical wrestlers of all time. Even in his post-ring days almost everything Race touched turned to gold like Lex Luger and Big Van Vader. Well almost everything – did someone say Yoshi Kwan?

The Fabulous Kangaroos: Before the Road Warriors and the Steiner Brothers there was Al Costello and Roy Heffernan, the team single-handedly responsible for putting tag team wrestling on the map. The Australian combo, complete in their bush hats, was the most dominating team throughout the 1950s and 60s. Years before 'Leapin' Lanny tossed his first frisbee it was the Kangaroos that were tossing boomerangs into the audience every night.

The Sheik: A true wrestling original, Ed Farhat is by some considered to be the true king of hardcore. An extreme pioneer, the Sheik was tossing fireballs and breaking every rule in the book even before his nephew Sabu was pooping in his first set of Arabian diapers. His most famous feud was with Bobo Brazil and it was one that lasted almost their entire violent careers. It is hard to say if the 'E-C-W' chants that rang out in a South Philly Bingo Hall during the late 1990s would have ever come to fruition if not for the violent nature that existed every time the Sheik mauled an opponent, especially when he was carving foreheads with a number two pencil.

Brute Bernard: The Canadian monster, seriously this guy is just outright mean-looking, is considered by many to be one of the greatest tag team wrestlers of all time. With a face for radio, the wild man took his uncontrollable in-ring style and formed a highly talented team with fellow bald northern neighbour Skull Murphy.

Stan Hansen: The double-tough Texan was an anti-hero in the form of Steve Austin, a hell-raising cowboy ready to knock your teeth out and not give a damn. His lariat clothesline 'broke necks' and with his psychotic persona and stiff work the badass from Borger, Texas, has been a major force all over the planet. Everyone from Hulk Hogan to Antonio Inoki has felt the wrath of the outspoken renegade. Even though he was a well-known commodity stateside, winning the AWA World Championship, his greatest legacy was created in the land of the rising sun.

Kevin Sullivan: Whenever you lead a stable called the Army of Darkness one thing is certain – you are guaranteed a spot in our 'Top 100 Heel in No Particular Order' list. As one of the darkest villains in history, Sullivan's work as the devil incarnate was pure evil. Among his many forays into the world of heel stables, the Boston-born bad guy was the leader of both the Varsity Club and the Dungeon of Doom. Sullivan was sick and sadistic, a true twisted talent in every sense of the word and who can forget the 'Tree of Woe'?

Brooklyn Brawler: Whether he's Steve Lombardi or the Brooklyn Brawler this guy has been losing matches for decades. This one-time member of the Heenan Family had a brief push back in the day and he even scored a clean victory over Triple H during The Game's heyday. However no wrestler in WWE history has been on the losing end of the 1-2-3 more times than the artist formerly known as Abe 'Knuckleball' Schwartz.

Mike Awesome: Regardless of his Fat Chick Thriller persona in the post-nWo WCW era we will always remember Mike Awesome for his victory over Masato Tanaka at ECW's One Night Stand PPV (which quite honestly in our eyes was the last ECW match ever). That 1970s guy was a versatile athlete able to powerbomb or hurl himself over the ropes and crush his opposition. The only time a contracted WCW star would defend the ECW title against a contracted WWE star was at an ECW event where Awesome lost the title to Taz, a historic yet controversial match for the ages.

The Moondogs: No relation to 'The Animal' George Marcin, the shaggy-haired, ripped-jean, bone-chewing Moondogs made their home town of Parts Unknown proud when they captured the WWE Tag Team Championship. When they were not chewing on their bones they were using them as weapons in the ring and for quite some time the team of Rex and Spot made quite the impression. Just curious – how old do you think Moondog Spot is in dog years?

Scott Steiner: As the All-American star from Michigan, Scott Steiner was part of a solid team with his brother Rick but before long the genetic freak traded in his older brother and his Frankensteiners for a bleached blonde look and membership into the nWo. Leaving the Dog-Faced Gremlin behind seemed to be a good career choice (even though they have re-formed in recent years) as he won most of WCW's championships before the doors were finally closed in 2001. The largest arms in the world matched with the biggest jackass in wrestling, 'Holla if ya agree with that!'

Wild Samoans: For 30 years Afa and Sika tore through opponents like they tore through raw fish during an interview segment. Managed by Captain Lou Albano, the three-time WWE title-holders set the bar high for Samoan wrestlers that have come before and after their Hall of Fame careers. Graduates of their highly regarded training centre include many top stars from yesterday and today: Yokozuna, Bam Bam Bigelow, Billy Kidman, Batista and yes even Gene Snitsky whose WWE career was about as useless as Sammy Davis Jr.'s glass eye. Snitsky aside, the Samoans were ahead of their time and a true treasure in the tag team division.

Ray Stevens: With Captain Lou Albano by his side, Ray Stevens was a can't-miss heel in WWE. His feud with Jimmy 'Superfly' Snuka was incredibly memorable, and in the years prior to that he was really a stud in the ring matching wits with Bruno Sammartino and 'crippling' opponents with fearless in-ring action – take his kneedrop finisher from the top rope for example. While he was a solo star, Stevens will arguably be best remembered as being part of a bunch of successful tag teams including the Blond Bombers with Pat Patterson but he was more than that and it's a shame he often flies under the radar.

Sgt. Slaughter: The man born Robert Remus was a long-time patriot and babyface until the Gulf War hit. In a ballsy move that was criticised, Sgt. Slaughter turned his back on the United States and WWE fans by becoming an Iraqi sympathiser on WWE TV – winning the WWE Championship and breaking hearts with each cobra clutch he put on good guys. While he sold the angle, we still prefer Sgt. as a babyface – heck, even today WWE occasionally dusts him off and puts him in a match against some new hot shot. That said, we applaud his effort as a heel – and hope to see a cameo from him in an upcoming terrible *G.I. Joe* movie sequel.

Bob Orton: When I was in third grade, I broke my arm and it took about six weeks to heal. In the case of 'Cowboy' Bob Orton, his broken arm or wrist or whatever it was lasted eons. Case in point: the grappler wore his cast for way too damn long. Realising that was just a storyline quirk, we'll drop that point and focus on what a damn good heel Orton was. A second-generation wrestler whose son Randy made it a trifecta, Orton made a name for himself first in NWA and then in WWE, where he was a main event heel. Early on, Orton really made his mark – taking on Hulk Hogan and other top faces, but eventually he was relegated to being a stooge for Roddy Piper. One wonders what would have happened had he continued going on as a singles wrestler instead of the *They Live* co-star's security chief, but we digress. Orton was still one of the best heels to come out of the 1970s and 1980s.

Rick Martel: It shouldn't have worked as well as it did, but boy did it. Following his stint tag-teaming with Tito Santana as the tandem Strike Force, Martel shed his babyface image and ushered in the era of 'The Model'. Always entertaining when it came to promos – especially when promoting his good looks and fake fragrance called Arrogance – the Quebec native was a pro in the ring who arguably gave better Boston crabs than a New England Legal Seafood restaurant. Years before turning heel with WWE, Martel was an accomplished babyface for the AWA – even winning the heavyweight title there – but he never really placed in the top tier in WWE, which is a shame. One look at his feud with Jake 'The Snake' Roberts alone, and you'll see what we're talking about. The man could do it all – in and out of the ring, and he did the impossible: he made the Can-Am Connection, a concept so cornball it might as well have been put together by Kelloggs, respectable.

Terry Funk: Every hardcore wrestler flocks to him, and puts him up on a pedestal – and for good reason. Terry Funk is a legend who ushered in a new era of hardcore wrestling, and grappled with greats like Ric Flair, Harley Race and Dusty Rhodes and still gets inside the squared circle as he approaches the big 7-0. The 'Funker' gave it his all no matter whether there were six, 60 or 6,000 people in an arena, and established himself as an uber-heel fairly early on – drawing more heat from a crowd than Taco Bell does an ass. A former NWA World Heavyweight Champion, the Texas native and his brother Dory are among the most talented men to ever get in a ring. But it's Terry Funk whose in-your-face style (cattle-branding stick anyone?) sets him apart from the rest. Added bonus? He appeared in *Road House* with Patrick Swayze, and his career remained unscathed.

'Sycho' Sid Vicious: Not many wrestlers can say they feuded with the likes of Robocop, El Gigante and Hulk Hogan, but than again Sid is not like most other wrestlers. Introduced in the late 1980s as a member of The Skyscrapers, the towering presence of the self-proclaimed 'ruler of the world' has headlined his fair share of pay-per-views over the past 25 years. The two-time WWE Champion's hell-raising earned him main event spots against two of the industry's most iconic figures (Hulk Hogan at WrestleMania VIII and the Undertaker at WrestleMania 13). The master of the powerbomb was an intimidating figure during his heyday which makes us wonder where his career would have been if he didn't trade in tossing jobbers from stretchers for tossing softballs in his home town of 'anywhere he damn well pleases' (no offence to residents of West Memphis, Arkansas). Sid's career was marred with its share of controversy and despite several title reigns and high-profile feuds some say his legacy and potential was never fully reached. Despite his heel runs however Sid always drew cheers from the crowd and his over-the-top in-your-face promos always made us want to root for one of the more imposing figures to ever set foot in the ring.

Jake 'The Snake' Roberts: Finishing moves in wrestling have come and gone but perhaps the most devastating of all is the DDT. Often imitated but never duplicated (never heard that one-liner before) the Jake Roberts DDT is one of the best finishers hands down. The snakeskin-boot-wearing grappler was not only known for shoving opponents' heads into the mat, he is also one of the greatest talkers in the history of the business. Unfortunately he is remembered for his high-profile personal problems but the native of Stone Mountain, Georgia, should be recognised most for his innovative in-ring work.

The guy carried around a snake and would drape it over hapless opponents after a victory and that's only the half of it. In one of the more heinous acts of villainy ever witnessed on a Saturday morning wrestling show the always-sinister Roberts introduced his king cobra to a helpless Randy Savage and the rest as they say is history. He may have unceremoniously ushered in the 'Austin 3:16' era but back in the day Jake Roberts was one badass mofo and in his prime would have given Stone Cold one hell of a damn fight.

Honky Tonk Man: It is still impossible to explain how Ricky Steamboat, one of the greatest in-ring performers of any era, was able to win arguably the greatest match in WrestleMania history yet he dropped the coveted Intercontinental Championship to what should have been a transitional title-holder at best in the Honky Tonk Man. However some 25-plus years later the world's most famous Elvis impersonator is still the longest-reigning IC champion in history (take that Santino's Honk-a-meter). Sure he got squashed and stunned by an over-the-top one-dimensional Ultimate Warrior but the Honky Tonk Man's greatest hits (guitar included) make him one of the most dangerous men to ever lace the wrestling boots. If you don't believe us just ask the Mega Powers. When he is not smashing gimmick guitars over opponents' heads to seal a cheap victory the cool, cocky and ba-ba-ba-bad star is as lethal as they come. Speaking of which you've got to be bad if you are able to convince Greg 'The Hammer' Valentine, a platinum blond subscriber for years, to go rogue and dye his golden locks jet black.

Skull Murphy: Any time your tag team partner is Killer Kowalski you're bound to show up on a top 100 heels of all time list. Of course when you're billed as Skull Murphy that is sure to help your cause. Skull was the consummate bad guy in the golden age of black and white television. His dreaded heart punch was essentially the kiss of death for many a good guy and his constant use of all objects, foreign or otherwise, was destined to become a thorn in any mild-mannered wrestler's side. The bald brute was best known as a tag specialist, capturing WWE tag gold with fellow crazy Canadian Brute Bernard. Sporting the bald guy look years before Steve Austin and Kurt Angle (sorry Nathan Jones) made the cue-ball famous, the notoriously dangerous Skull Murphy was winning gold and causing in-ring treachery for several dominating years.

'Ravishing' Rick Rude: On a historic November night during the heart of the Monday Night Wars the self-proclaimed 'Sexiest Man Alive' shocked the wrestling world when he appeared on *WWE Raw* as a member of D-Generation X and on *WCW Monday Nitro* as a member of the nWo all during the same evening. Of course we shouldn't be surprised, as the Ravishing one always seemed to beat to the sound of his own drum. As a main member of the hated Heenan Family, Rude's pre-ring work left audiences in a fit when he would demand and invite fans to observe what a real man looked like. His matches were filled with plenty of in-ring posing and usually ended with his 'Rude Awakening' neckbreaker backed by a kiss for a lucky lady in the crowd. Despite his cocky attitude and constant chip on the shoulder the moustachioed superstar was indeed an incredible in-ring competitor. With a posthumous Hall of Fame induction in his future (we hope) we will never forget his Cheryl Roberts-inspired ring trunks or his Bobby the Brain-guided victory over the Ultimate Warrior for the Intercontinental Championship at WrestleMania V – that was simply ravishing.

Dick the Bruiser: Not only did the tough as nails Nevada native earn the reputation as 'The World's Most Dangerous Wrestler' he is also credited with coining one of the wrestling world's most unforgettable nicknames. As legend has it the Bruiser was the first person to call Bobby 'The Brain' Heenan 'The Weasel'. The former Green Bay Packer made the jump to the squared circle in the mid-1950s, trading in his helmet and shoulder pads for a pair of black trunks and matching boots. The field may have changed but for Bruiser the results were the same and bones were sure to be broken. The gravelly-voiced tough guy was in charge of the World Wrestling Association, which ran alongside the much larger AWA promotion that was led by Vern Gagne. It was here that Dick (no relation to Chip) the Bruiser became a one-time holder of the world championship as well as a five-time holder of the tag team championship with his partner The Crusher. He never met a broken bone he didn't like and for that the former gridiron bully is sure to crack any and all top heel lists making the rounds.

Kevin Nash: From bodyguard to Big Sexy, the multi-time world champion has been a major part of the wrestling landscape over the last two decades. After once eliminating seven superstars in less than 18 minutes during a Royal Rumble match his star shone even brighter when he defeated Bob Backlund in only eight seconds to become WWE Champion. He once tore the prosthetic leg off of WWE Hall of Famer Mad Dog Vachon and used it as a weapon against his on-off BFF Shawn Michaels. Never without controversy, the former Diesel traded in his Titan Towers membership card and set his sights on the greener pastures of WCW where he became a founding member of the nWo. As part of the Outsiders he helped Hulk Hogan turn 'Hollywood' and at one time even used Rey Mysterio as a human lawn dart. Years removed from the Vinny Vegas era, big Kev and his colleagues ran roughshod over an entire company and helped revolutionise the industry as we know it. The always brash and controversial big man, when he is not jobbing to the Fingerpoke of Doom, is backing up his boasts with a jack-knife powerbomb or two – and in his own words that's just too sweet!

The Miz: It has been well documented that for a few decades MTV played music videos. VJs like J.J. Jackson, 'Downtown' Julie Brown ('we saw your boobs' – hat nod to Seth MacFarlane), and wet-fart Jesse Camp used to intro the freshest, hippest songs in all the land. Heck, they even introduced us to the musical side of Eddie Murphy with his immortal anthem 'Party All The Time'. Nothing beats the cameo from Rick James in which he nods uncontrollably each time Murphy fails to hit a note.

But we digress. In the late 1990s and throughout the 2000s, the once music-only television network was focused on reality shows and why wouldn't it? MTV birthed the first with *The Real World*, an unscripted, groundbreaking drama about strangers who are thrown together in a city apartment to fight, screw, and screw each other over. Michael Mizanin appeared on the series in its tenth season, and by far, he has found the most success post-series.

Following his run as a likable jock, the Ohio native appeared on various MTV reality series before trying out for WWE's *Tough Enough*. While he lost to Daniel Pudder (Google him, and you'll quickly learn you have no idea who Daniel Pudder is), he caught the eye of company trainers and worked his ass off to make it in the 'big leagues'. Boy did he ever. Taking a page from his 'Miz' character, which he perfected on *The Real World*, Mizanin quickly made an impact on WWE TV, winning the tag belts with John Morrison, and going on to win the US title as well. He also held the tag titles with Big Show, but the fact they referred to themselves as ShoMiz loses key street cred and doesn't deserve another sentence. In 2010, The Miz won the Money in the Bank ladder match, and cashed in his contract to snag the WWE Championship from Randy Orton.

He spent over five months as champion, which in the current wrestling climate is probably equal to 15 years if it was the 1980s. In any event, The Miz remains a top grappler in the company – moving from heel to face with precision, but we like him better as a bad guy. His impeccable mic skills evoke the golden years of wresting, and his in-ring skill is all kinds of awesome. For that, and for so many other reasons, he easily places in our top 100. If our next book is about top douches in pop culture, we'll be sure to reserve a spot for Puck.

Ric Flair: Limousine riding, jet flying, kiss stealing, yes, and if you made it this far you already know what it takes to get to the top of space mountain or in this case the number one spot on our all-time heels of wrestling list. For over 35 years the Nature Boy has been 'the man' and his 16 world championships and not one but two inductions into the WWE Hall of Fame are just the icing on the Slick Ric cake…wooooo! The Dirtiest Player in the Game is not just a nickname; honestly what else would you call a guy who is synonymous with the nut shot? With his bleached blond dew to go along with his custom-made suits and Rolex collection, 'the Champ' has been in the ring with the best (Rugged Ronnie Garvin not so much) and has always managed to find a way to win. We give him a pass for the Black Scorpion debacle and reward him for being the only man to ever win the WWE Championship in a Royal Rumble match. He led the Four Horsemen and to this day the Nature Boy continues to style and profile for all new generations of wrestling fans. OK, why not, here is another one…woooooo!

Greg 'The Hammer' Valentine: The 1990s started off with a bang for Stanley Kirk Burrell, AKA MC Hammer. The rapper became a sensation with his *Please Hammer Don't Hurt 'Em* album, spawning hit singles like 'U Can't Touch This', 'Pray', and 'Have You Seen Her'. More importantly to pop culture, he spawned trends like baggy pants, fancy specs, and a wee-small ponytail in the back of his Hammer head.

Whereas MC Hammer dominated the early 1990s, another Hammer dominated the 1980s and we're not talking about that gumshoe Mike Hammer. Greg 'The Hammer' Valentine was a chip off the old block. The son of wrestler Johnny Valentine made a name for himself in the business, winning the NWA United States Heavyweight Championship, and the WWE Intercontinental Championship – to name two. Who could forget his memorable match (and count-out) against Junkyard Dog in the inaugural WrestleMania? Speaking of which, he carried that title for nine months, which was about as long as Mae Young carried that hand.

While he was a memorable singles wrestler, Valentine is often associated with tag teams he was a part of, and rightfully so.

Superstar Billy Graham: If you can look past the fake karate gimmick he used during his early 1980s comeback and forget about his cringe watching meatball parm-looking hip surgery shown on a Saturday morning WWE programme back in the day then what you've got is one of the most charismatic and trend-setting rule-breakers of all time. He transcended pop culture with his innovative catchphrases and unique look that helped set the stage for guys like Jesse 'The Body' Ventura, 'Big Poppa Pump' Scott Steiner and even 'Hollywood' Hulk Hogan himself. Managed by the legendary Grand Wizard, the Reflection of Perfection captured the WWE Championship from

Bruno Sammartino and from there he electrified the world and sold out Madison Square Garden as the industry's top heel. The Sensation of the Nation, the Number One Creation, he was one of a kind and surely a superstar among the stars.

Kamala: Face paint has a storied history in the world of wrestling. The Missing Link found it easy being green. The Ultimate Warrior scored with his multi-coloured arch around his eyes. Sting resonated a Warrior look then an Eric Draven knock-off in WCW followed by a Joker rip-off in TNA. There are countless examples of this, but only one star had the audacity to use body paint to iconic levels, and we're not talking about the slop Jeff Hardy tosses on himself.

Two stars and a moon. Need we say more? In the world of wrestling no other grappler in history has had a more memorable belly than Kamala. With two stars on his – to quote *Fight Club* – 'bitch tits' and a moon around his belly, the Ugandan Giant made an impact right off the bat with his original gimmick, which also included a leopard-print loincloth that looked as if it was taken from Jimmy Snuka's closet circa 1987 or, um, today.

Kamala, whose real name is James Harris, apparently grew up in Mississippi, but his gimmick took him to Africa – an idea which, according to Wikipedia, came from two Jerrys (Jarrett and Lawler). Kamala wrestled for many organisations before landing in WWE in 1984, and jumped around like House of Pain a bit throughout his career. A memorable heel who wrestled bare-foot and made uncontrollably obnoxious sounds in the ring, Kamala drew instant heat thanks to his ring work and valets which included Freddie Blassie, The Wizard, and the enigmatic masked man Kim Chee. Throughout his many runs in WWE, Kamala battled stars like Andre the Giant, Hulk Hogan, and Jake 'The Snake' Roberts. He might not have been the most athletic wrestler of all time, but he made his mark as a main event heel thanks to his 'Air Africa' splash, back-handed chops, and memorable headbutts and butt kicks.

Other highlights included eating a live chicken on *Tuesday Night Titans* only not really, wrestling the Undertaker in a coffin match at 1992's Survivor Series, and being scared shitless of snakes when he feuded with Roberts. While he went on to become a reliable face (we'll remind you to Google Slick teaching him to bowl), we always preferred our Ugandan Giant as a bad guy, flapping his belly loudly with his hands, and letting his legacy speak for itself…figuratively. Because, you know, he didn't talk.

Nikolai Volkoff: Maybe one day the creators of *Men Are From Mars, Women Are From Venus* will pen a follow-up called *Josip Peruzović Is From Croatia, Nikolai Volkoff Is From Russia*. Don't count on it, but perhaps that title would be the first words in a Nikolai Volkoff autobiography. The epitome of the words 'instant heat', the WWE gave Peruzović a Russian identity (he is half-

Russian actually) and paired him with an Iranian and thus, a legendary tag team was born with he and the Iron Sheik. It is hard to believe he actually debuted in WWE with Captain Lou Albano in his corner in the early 1970s under the moniker Bepo Mongol. It is also hard to believe anyone thought up the name Bepo Mongol but anyway.

Volkoff had runs in the AWA and Mid-Atlantic, and feuded with Bruno Sammartino when he returned to WWE in the mid-1970s, but who are we kidding, even though he had an impressive solo career, he really made it when he teamed with the Iron Sheik. A master of orchestrating heat, who could forget him singing the Soviet national anthem before every match?

Volkoff had many highlights throughout his career in tag and singles competition – thanks in large to his anti-USA gimmick and signature Boston crab and bearhugs. He also had some 'WTF' moments like that zany flag match against Corporal Kirchner at WrestleMania II and his run with the Bolsheviks, but those exploits can be covered in another book. When you put his career together, he really was one of the most recognisable heels in the history of 1980s WWE. Plus, he played a scene-stealer in the 'Land of a Thousand Dances' and Cyndi Lauper's 'Goonies R Good Enough' music videos, which was probably pretty cool to tell hot chicks at parties.

Jim Cornette: As the leader of the Midnight Express the loudmouth from Louisville, Kentucky, is one of the most controversial managers to ever carry a tennis racket to the ring. OK, never mind, he was the only manager to ever carry a tennis racket to the ring. As outspoken as they come, the momma's boy managed both versions of the Midnight Express to numerous gold runs and legendary feuds along the way. He once blew out his knee falling from a scaffold during a tag match between the Midnight Express and the Road Warriors and years later he even made a tag team of Bart Gunn and Bob Holly (mid-carders at best) seem somewhat legit and hip. Helping derail the Lex Express in the early 1990s as the 'American spokesperson' for Yokozuna was one of his greatest gifts to rule-breaking and for several years later he continued to raise hell both in the ring and behind the curtain.

Nikita Koloff: During the height of the Cold War the Russian Nightmare was introduced to a wrestling audience as a ruthless Soviet machine hell-bent on dominating the National Wrestling Alliance and a locker room full of silly American wrestlers. Brought to the states by his Uncle Ivan, the 'evil Russian' did not disappoint. With limited in-ring experience Koloff was still a great sell and his devastating 'Russian Sickle' clothesline was a very formidable finisher, just ask Magnum T.A. or any jobber who fought in Atlanta, Georgia, at 6.05pm on a Saturday back in the late 1980s.

Blackjack Mulligan: One of the toughest dudes to ever step in the ring, Mulligan played the part of an outlaw cowboy ready to fight at the drop of a dime. With his black handlebar bert (that's a moustache in our eyes kids), black trunks, and black glove, Blackjack's black heart was certainly full of hatred. He feuded with the likes of Pedro Morales, Bruno Sammartino and Haystacks Calhoun. Straight from a movie western, so it seemed, he later formed a tag team with Blackjack Lanza which won the WWE Tag Team Championship and eventually he was given the ultimate career honour of being inducted into the Hall of Fame. Wrestling is in his blood and his influence stands strong yesterday and today in the form of his sons Barry and Kendall Windham, his son-in-law Mike Rotundo and his grandson Bray Wyatt.

Killer Kowalski: No relation to Killer Jones, Kowalski is one of the most hated villains of all time and he solidified his reputation when he tore off a piece of Yukon Eric's ear while dropping a knee. He was a menacing figure in the ring but a gentle soul out of it. He feuded with Bruno Sammartino (who didn't feud with Sammartino?) and he won the WWE tag titles with Big John Studd dressed in black masks and known as The Executioners (1 and 2). After his days as a rule-breaker wound down he opened the Kowalski Wrestling School and alumni include Triple H, The Eliminators, Chris Nowinski, Damien Sandow and Fandango.

Karl Von Hess: Can you imagine if any current wrestlers caused near riots? Not only would it be a

YouTube sensation it would also be trending worldwide on Twitter. Fortunately for Karl Von Hess the character he played of a Nazi sympathiser on the black and white televisions of yesteryear was not created during a time of media and social networking. Von Hess was the first character in the post-war era to 'support' the Third Reich and although he was shot at he drew heat and sold out crowds wherever he went. Von Hess would not have been a fan of *Inglourious Basterds* but who are we to judge, we would pay to see the ruthless German against Quentin's fictitious Donny Donowitz any day of the week. Go get 'em bear!

Johnny Valentine: For close to nearly three decades Greg's dad brought his brash arrogance to the ring and was clearly one of the most hated stars of his era. He had the look of a cocky and confident champion with his bleached blond hair (still a staple among today's stars, just go and ask Dolph Ziggler) and his amazing physique. He built quite the legacy and few if any can match his huge success in the squared circle.

Muhammad Hassan: In one year, bad timing and poor taste came together and brought us Mark Copani's Muhammad Hassan character in WWE. In what could best be described as an update of the Iron Sheik's Iraqi sympathiser turn alongside Sgt. Slaughter at the time of the Gulf War but in a far more dangerous and scary world serving as its backdrop, the Hassan gimmick went the way of the buffalo far too soon.

Hassan debuted at a time in which terror alert levels were told in colours. After a strong build-up to his controversial arrival, Hassan was thrown into the big show right off the bat in 2004 and knocked it out of the park with his performance. Advocating against media stereotypes against Middle Easterners in the post-9/11 world and more, he and his manager Daivari drew instant heat. In his first year, Hassan beat top faces like Chris Jericho and The Hurricane and had tagged with Daivari to take on Shawn Michaels and Hulk Hogan at the Backlash pay-per-view. Hassan also feuded with Batista for a bit, but it all came to an abrupt end in the summer of 2005 during a feud with the Undertaker, which culminated with a loss at The Great American Bash.

A few weeks before that PPV, at a *SmackDown* taping which aired on 4 July with a disclaimer, 'Taker beat Daivari but Hassan started praying and five men in black shirts and ski-masks appeared and attacked the Phenom. Three days after that episode was shown, the London bombings took place. Since the episode aired anyway, WWE was criticised and reportedly the UPN, which aired the programme, wanted him off.

Eventually, WWE released Copani and the Muhammad Hassan character and his camel clutch were sent packing. We wonder what might have been because the Italian-born Copani sold the gimmick so well, and backed it up with solid ring and mic skills. We understand the timing was wrong, and the gimmick was in poor taste, but when it comes to the best heels over the past decade, Hassan easily places in the top ten.

Mr Fuji: Mr T, Mr Ed, Mr Hooper, and Mr Roper. OK, you get the picture, the world has seen its fair share of Misters. Even the wrestling world has gone on to pay homage to the courteous title for those rugged gents in our lives i.e. Mr Hughes, Mr Wresting II and Mr Saito. But none of these men or horses – yes that's right we are calling you out Mr Ed (how is that for a heel turn?) – can hold a candle to the unforgettable banzai-dropping, salt-tossing Mr Fuji. Regarded as one of the most dangerous men in the biz (as Tiger Chung Lee gently weeps) Fuji captured tag gold five times as a wrestler and even managed the likes of Demolition and the Powers of Pain to prominent tag team success. Clad in his trademark tuxedo and bowler hat, the 'Fuji Vice' star was a staple in the 1980s wrestling boom but among his greatest claims to fame was leading the great Yokozuna to multiple WWE Championships.

Nailz: OK, so maybe this guy should be in the top 50 biggest busts in wrestling because his wrestling shelf-life lasted less than Little Beaver in a mixed six-man tag match. That being said, we would never forget the brief but brutal career of Nailz. In all his orange prison jumpsuit glory, aka the worst wrestling gear this side of John Cena's jean shorts, the former convict turned grappler made his presence felt by attacking his former prison guard Big Bossman. Of course the one-time Mr Magnificent was part of the first and only ever nightstick match which he shockingly lost but regardless of his Survivor Series jobbing, this book has done its best to keep the Cobb County jailbird relevant for at least one last run and somewhere a guy named Kevin Wacholz will thank us but seriously dude smile, what did you do anyway that got you into all this trouble in the first place?

Hulk Hogan: John Cena and WWE could learn a thing or two from what Hulk Hogan and WCW did back in 1996. At the time, and for just about 15 years prior to it, the Hulkster had been the go-to babyface in the industry. He was on *Sports Illustrated* covers, in bad movies, TV shows like *The Tonight Show* with Johnny Carson, and was the poster boy for an industry that very much needed a poster boy. In many ways, Hogan put pro wrestling on the mainstream map. Hogan left WWE in 1994 for WCW and shocked the wrestling world and changed the industry landscape forever.

But, again Hogan was the good guy there. With a new 'American Made' theme song, Hulkamania ran wild in the Ted Turner company, but it was still the same red-and-yellow good-guy gimmick. By 1996, sensing his image was growing stale, the wrestling world got turned upside down when – for the first time since he reached such great heights – Hogan turned heel at the Bash at the Beach pay-per-view.

The way in which the storyline played out was a thing of perfection. With Scott Hall and Kevin

Nash defecting from WWE for WCW on its *Nitro* programme in previous weeks, they built up that a third member would be arriving at the Bash. When the third member was revealed to be Hogan (he turned on 'Macho Man' Randy Savage in the ring), the New World Order was born and the fans went bat-shit crazy.

The nWo had a strong run for a few years, and despite it losing its lustre (Scott Norton really?), Hogan's new badass 'Hollywood' Hogan character – with his black face paint outlining his trademark Twinkie-stache and new intro music ('Voodoo Chile' by Jimi Hendrix) – was always appealing and never got stale like that 'American Made' song did.

True, fans hated the fact he turned his backs on the very people who trained, said their prayers, and took their vitamins, but Hogan sold being a heel as well as he sold being a good guy. And brother, that's the stuff of legends.

Eric Bischoff: One of the greatest minds to ever be involved in pro wrestling. The former executive producer and president of WCW changed the wrestling landscape for the better when he was put in charge of WCW's *Monday Nitro* and pitted it against competitor WWE's *Raw is War*.

Bischoff, who actually got his start in the American Wrestling Association, was an out-of-the-box thinker who joined WCW as an announcer in 1991. By 1994, he was executive vice-president of the company, and recruited Hulk Hogan. By the late 1990s, Bischoff was president of the company and brought on Scott Hall, Kevin Nash, and countless other WWE veterans – thus creating a war between the two companies – especially when the New World Order debuted with Hogan tagging with Nash and Hall as part of a takeover storyline with WCW. With that, WCW bested WWE in the ratings and stayed there for a few years.

On the air, Bischoff became a reliable heel manager for the nWo as 'Eazy E'. We all know by now that WCW would eventually shit the proverbial bed, and Vince McMahon would purchase the company by 2001. But, Bischoff's on-air bastardry and calculated, ruthless game-changing ways behind the scenes make him one of the best heel personalities ever.

Furthermore, he solidified that with a memorable stint in WWE as the *Raw* general manager from 2002–2005. While he has had stints in TNA Impact Wrestling, we miss Bischoff on the grand scale he deserves. He has never appeared live on a WrestleMania event and deserves to be in the WWE Hall of Fame. Fingers crossed it'll happen one day and when it does, hell will officially have frozen over. That said, it has before in this industry thanks to Eazy E.

One Man Gang: When not Akeem, George Gray was a captivating bad guy as One Man Gang – working various main events, notably against Hulk Hogan. Famous for his mohawk, and the 747 Splash finisher, he was a badass heel even though Akeem was a badass gimmick.

Scott Hall: Hey yo! Despite the fact he ripped off Al Pacino's *Scarface* gimmick, Hall was a solid and always entertaining heel whether he went by his own name or as Razor Ramon. We will look past the denim-on-denim look he used in WCW, because he was an integral part of the nWo and the Monday Night Wars.

Kane: He is not pretty to look at with his mask on or off, but there's no question Undertaker's 'brother' has had a significant career in the industry. The fact he survived the Katie Vick storyline is a testament to his legs in this business. His Big Red Machine gimmick sure beats the evil dentist he used to play on TV. So wait, is Percy Pringle/Paul Bearer really his dad?

John Bradshaw Layfield (JBL): He was one tough son-of-a-bitch with the APA along with Ron Simmons, but JBL really carved a niche in the industry with his rich cowboy gimmick in the 2000s. A solid main eventer and current announcer, watching him in the ring was like watching J.R. Ewing in his prime.

Kurt Angle: While we prefer him goofier than his ultra-serious persona, Angle has excelled at every single level in the business for both WWE (small sheriff hat and all) and TNA Impact Wrestling. His matches against Chris Benoit in particular were always breathtaking. Oh, it's true…it's damn true.

Brock Lesnar: The Next Big Thing actually lived up to the hype when he debuted on *Monday Night Raw* in 2002 following WrestleMania XVIII. Lesnar's F5 of Al Snow set the tone, and having Paul Heyman as his manager was a stroke of genius. Sure he went all MMA on us, but we're happy he's back – at least if you're reading this in 2014.

Paul Heyman: He started the extreme revolution with ECW – years after he was seen flaunting his Zach Morris cellphone in WCW, and has brought his A-game on-and-off in the WWE as an announcer and manager. His talent and smarts almost make up for the fact he's a bald grown man with a ponytail.

Jimmy Hart: The Mouth of the South used to have heart boxer shorts on whenever a wrestler embarrassed him after a match. That takes dedication.

With his dopey megaphone and his irritating southern accent, Hart did the impossible: he made you like him. One of the best managers ever to grace the ring (with arguably the worst blazers you've ever seen), Hart managed greats like the Hart Foundation, Jerry Lawler, Honky Tonk Man, the Fabulous Rougeaus, and Adrian Adonis.

Ted DiBiase: The Million Dollar Man created his own belt, tried to buy the WWE Championship, and used to stuff money in guys' mouths. Arguably the personification of the 1980s decade in which he wrestled, DiBiase was all about greed…and Virgil, but more so greed.

Bret Hart: While he switched from face to heel many times in his career, we actually found ourselves rooting more for Bret the bad guy than Bret the good guy. With terribly cheesy sunglasses and soul-glow hair, Hart became one of the biggest wrestlers of all time. His infamous 'Bret got screwed' match against Shawn Michaels in Montreal is still the stuff of legend. Heck, he even made pink look cool.

Adrian Adonis: Not everyone could sell the 'Adorable' gimmick the way Adrian Adonis did back in the 1980s – well, Vanity Smurf might have been able to if he was real. Decades before *Brokeback* cowboys and groundbreaking Supreme Court decisions, Adonis and his Flower Shop gimmick – clearly inspired by Gorgeous George – changed the wrestling world forever.

King Kong Bundy: The grappler known as King Kong Bundy is currently a stand-up comedian, but in the 1980s, there was nothing funny about the persona Chris Pallies created with his larger-than-life bad-guy character. Some highlights included his 'Avalanche' and five-count finisher, co-headlining WrestleMania II against Hulk Hogan in a steel cage, and appearing on *Married with Children*, which is probably on his IMDB credits.

Yokozuna: Stereotypes be damned, this heel – arguably the biggest in the literal sense – held his own (and then some) against the likes of Bret Hart, Hulk Hogan, and Lex Luger. His time on this planet was all too brief, but his waist was all too large. Banzai!

Owen Hart: The King of Harts held several titles in the world of wrestling (he held tag belts with Yokozuna, Jeff Jarrett, and Davey Boy Smith), and would have likely had more had his life not been tragically cut short. We always preferred him as a bad guy as opposed to a blue guy.

Captain Lou Albano: He had a great run as a wrestler, but we prefer to remember the rubber-banded tough guy as a heel manager. From his work with Ray Stevens to his later days managing the Wild Samoans, Albano was always outspoken and really a true original in the business. You have got to be pretty bad to pin rubber bands to your face, right? Hold on, let's call Cyndi Lauper.

Triple H: The Game will never be over because he's a McMahon, and that's probably a good thing. The Cerebral Assassin as he has often been called has always excelled on the mic and in the ring, and did the near impossible: he made us forget about that terrible aristocratic character he played before he started spewing water outside the ropes. We will give you a mulligan for Chyna.

The Rock: Dwayne Johnson was primarily a good guy during his years in WWE, but when he was bad, he sold it like the box office champ he is. He had numerous feuds with babyfaces, but we'll single out the second match he had against Hulk Hogan as a favourite. Oh, and his whole gimmick launched the *SmackDown* franchise, and that show's title surprisingly outlasted the WWE Restaurant in New York City which had long outlasted the Nitro Grill. What is he cooking anyway?

'Stone Cold' Steve Austin: It is difficult to single him out as a bad guy, because he was in his own league, but how do you have any wrestling list and leave the Texas Rattlesnake out of the mix? The answer? You can't.

Edge: Whether it was lip-locking Lita in front of her ex, Matt Hardy, or spearing a host of really good guys, Edge quickly carved his name in wrestling history. Had it not been for a forced medical retirement, the Rated R Superstar might have won a couple more titles. At the very least, he may have Frenched Vicki Guerrero some more. Oh you think you know me?

Goldust: The most original heel ever – especially any who ever put on make-up and a gold bodysuit, Dustin Runnels lived up to his father's legacy by creating memorable matches and even more memorable promos. That said, he was stripped down to his lingerie at a WrestleMania match.

'Macho Man' Randy Savage: Not many men can say that they ran neck and neck with Hulk Hogan during the 1980s and in fact only one can claim he did just that. He is one of the most colourful and charismatic wrestlers ever. 'Macho Man' Randy Savage, with his raspy voice and signature ring attire, helped usher in an era of wrestling that is still being played out to this very day. 'Ohhh yeaahh' was his catchphrase every time the six-time champion wanted to get his point across. A major pay-per-view player, Savage has headlined everything from WrestleMania to Starrcade.

He was as entertaining out of the ring as he was in it. The pride of Sarasota, Florida, made his splash upon his arrival in WWE after choosing Miss Elizabeth to be his valet, turning down the services of established managers such as Jimmy Hart and 'Classy' Freddy Blassie. He broke the rule-breaking mould and he solidified it when he used a stashed foreign object to help capture the Intercontinental Championship from Tito Santana. His match with Ricky Steamboat at WrestleMania III is regarded as one of the greatest ever. The sky was the limit for the Macho Man, briefly the Macho King after winning the King of the Ring tournament in 1987, as he captured the WWE Championship, he made and destroyed a relationship with Hulk Hogan, he was a solid colour commentator for a bit, he joined WCW and through all that he even had time to snap into a Slim Jim when the opportunity presented itself. The Macho Man will surely be missed but the Madness will live on forever.

Shawn Michaels: The Heartbreak Kid broke a lot of hearts when he super-kicked Marty Jannetty through the Barber Shop window. Having said that, he should be praised because the Rockers was a terrible gimmick. They were rocking all right – but less AC/DC and more nursing home rocking chair. In all seriousness, arguably no superstar has had the career Michaels has and while he has mainly been a babyface for the past decade or so, he was a wonderful prick in the 1990s.

Eddie Guerrero: Lie. Cheat. Steal. Eddie Guerrero did all of this to get a win, but before he did that in WWE, he founded the Latino World Order in WCW. OK, let's start over. Guerrero was one of the best heels to grace the wrestling world, and his death probably hit WWE programming the hardest – well, at least the writers' room. Guerrero was money. WWE is still looking for a worthy heel to fill his big shoes.

Bobby 'The Brain' Heenan: The best manager in the history of wrestling. The best announcer in the history of wrestling. The best ensemble of talent any manager has ever had. He was the funniest, most entertaining personality that has been in this industry. And he could take a bump like no other weasel could. They broke the mould when they created Bobby 'The Brain' Heenan. Heck, even his LJN action figure was cool.

Diamond Dallas Page: Call this one a heel turn by us – DDP was mostly a good guy in WCW, but when he debuted in WWE he was shockingly revealed to be the Undertaker's stalker in a major, built-up storyline. Well, at least his intro music sounded like 'Smells Like Teen Spirit', and he has great teeth.

Lance Storm: Lance Storm played his stoic personality to a tee in WCW, ECW and WWE, but we weren't drawn to his character. Trained in Stu Hart's dojo, Storm was among the best physical wrestlers to hit the ring in the 1990s and 2000s. Cloudy with a Chance of Meatballs? No, clear skies whenever Storm was in the ring. Save me a breadstick.

Sherri Martel: If Miss Elizabeth was the beauty queen in the wrestling world, 'Sensational' Sherri Martel was the beauty school drop-out – and a conniving one at that. While she made her mark as a wrestler (Google her matches against the Fabulous Moolah), Martel really took off as a manager for the likes of Randy Savage, Ric Flair, and Shawn Michaels. The former Sensational Queen always chewed scenery with her ruthless bitchiness, bizarre make-up and outfits, and is arguably the most successful female manager of all time.

Jim 'The Anvil' Neidhart: Often overshadowed by his tag team partner Bret Hart and other superstars of the pre-Doink wrestling era, Jim 'The Anvil' Neidhart was a reliable heel in the 1980s and 1990s – breaking from the pack with his signature goatee, sinister laugh, and over-the-top promos. While he has fallen on hard times – like so many grapplers of his day – we remember Neidhart as not only one half of one of the most successful tag teams in wrestling history (the Hart Foundation), but one of the most entertaining.

Paul Orndorff: When Paul Orndorff turned on his friend and tag team partner Hulk Hogan in the early 1980s, he became the company's top heel. For those who followed his career beforehand, it came as little surprise. In the NWA, Orndorff tagged with Jimmy Snuka and took flight in the Georgia territory as well. Orndorff was the total package – he had a killer bod, decent mic skills, and perfected the piledriver like no other before him. Mr Wonderful was just that – pretty damn wonderful.

William Regal: When you think of the top heels in wrestling, William Regal is probably not the guy who comes to mind right away. But he makes our list because no other *Raw* commissioner or general manager resonated as much as Regal did. The Brit, who was the first member of Vince McMahon's Kiss My Ass Club, had moments of brilliance as an in-ring competitor but we preferred him running the show on Monday nights – specifically with Tajiri. His promos with the Japanese hardcore grappler were classic.

Brian Pillman: He burst on to the scene with an arsenal of aerial moves and backed by his missile dropkick and tiger-striped undies, the former gridiron star turned Flyin' Brian was a mainstay in WCW's light heavyweight division. Soon however he formed a tag team and friendship with 'Stunning' Steve Austin and the two became known as the Hollywood Blonds. They took rule-breaking by the horns, quickly becoming one of the best teams in the business. When the Blonds eventually split Pillman was once again fighting against the forces of evil but sooner rather than later he found a home as part of the Four Horsemen. It was during this time that his unpredictable behaviour and infamous worked shoots catapulted his career and made him into one of wrestling's hottest commodities. He was 'fired' from WCW for calling out Kevin Sullivan, he came this close (thumb and pointer finger almost touching) to whipping it out and urinating in an ECW ring and, speaking of whipping it out, he remains the only wrestling personality ever to pull out a gun on live television. A Loose Cannon indeed.

Larry Zbyszko: The former tag team champion was the protégé of Bruno Sammartino. He was a crowd favourite until he brutally attacked his mentor during a technical exhibition match, which still rates as one of the most shocking heel turns of all time. The vicious attack culminated in the much-anticipated Showdown At Shea. After leaving WWE the Real Living Legend excelled in the AWA and WCW respectively before finally landing behind the microphone and quickly becoming the most annoying thing on *Nitro* besides Mongo McMichael's Pepe.

The Undertaker: Streaks are meant to be broken unless your name is Mark Calaway. The man better known to wrestling fans as the Undertaker has never lost a match at WrestleMania, and while his 21-0 record is astonishing, his career is more than just a set of numbers. Ever since he made his debut in 1990, the Phenom has been a fan favourite – face, heel or 'tweener. Surprisingly agile for a big man, 'Taker has excelled against a who's who of WWE Hall of Famers past, present, and future including Hulk Hogan, Jimmy Snuka, Triple H, The Rock, King Kong Bundy and Shawn Michaels. His infamous Hell in a Cell match on 28 June 1998 gains buzz even today because Mankind fell from the top of the cage, but watch the match again and you'll see just how well the two battled. Undertaker gives it his all whether he is doing a house show or a pay-per-view. That is why he is so respected in the industry, and by his peers. Even when he was repackaged as the American Bad Ass, 'Taker sold his image to fans and made them root hard for him – bandana and motorcycle be damned. It is only a matter of time before 'Taker gets inducted into the WWE Hall of Fame, but he doesn't seem ready to retire the Deadman gimmick any time soon. Our best guess? He will finish when he gets to 25-0 at 'Mania.

Dolph Ziggler: The Ohio native may have a name that rips off the leading member of *Boogie Nights*, but there is no mistaking the raw natural talent Nicholas Nemeth has as Dolph Ziggler. Formerly with the ill-constructed Spirit Squad, Ziggler emerged as a top heel in the company thanks to his alliance with Vickie Guerrero. A former Intercontinental and US champ, he had his first World Heavyweight Championship reign in 2011. We expect more from this bleached-blond charismatic badass in the near future.

Demolition: Collectively, Demolition were a kick-ass tandem. Sure, the face-painted heels were nothing more than a Road Warriors clone, but Bill Eadie and Barry Darsow made the most of their Ax and Smash characters so much so that they're probably one of the top three tag teams in WWE history – at least pre-1995. If only they had never expanded to three members…that was when they jumped the ring shark.

CM Punk: Since bursting on to the scene after a successful run in the indies the Second City Saint has proven time and again that perhaps he is the very best in the world. Since he threatened to leave WWE following his controversial 'pipe bomb' tirade in which he took shots at the entire McMahon family in the summer of 2011, the Chicago-made superstar has raised his game to unbelievably new heights. After winning the WWE Championship Punk did leave the company only to return to become the 'voice of the voiceless' and the unofficial spokesman for the defunct WWE ice cream bar. His in-ring psychology is second to none and his record-setting championship run only speaks for itself. As he hears the cheers, especially from his home-town fans, it is no surprise that Punk has proven to be one of the top heels of the modern era. The sky is the limit and with two Money in the Bank briefcases cashed in already the Straight Edge star has plenty of time to prove why he is the best wrestler on the planet.

Buddy Rogers: To say Buddy Rogers inspired a generation of wrestlers is an understatement. Take Ric Flair for instance who took Buddy's look, his pompous attitude, his finishing hold and even his

---

Ricky Steamboat's Top Heels and Matches

1. Ric Flair gave me my first real break in the business. He taught me a lot in the ring.

2. Randy Savage – WrestleMania III was the best match of my career…taught me how everything must be perfect.

3. Jake Roberts – what a technician in the ring.

4. Don Muraco – for a big guy, he could go! Twenty-five minutes into the match, and he's bump'n and feed'n like a lightweight! He taught me how to slow down and let each moment breathe.

nickname, the Nature Boy. This was a testament to Rogers's career which was filled with championship accolades and plenty of showmanship. The two-time world champion helped usher in television with the likes of Lou Thesz and 'Handsome' Johnny Barend. He was charismatic and downright smug when it came to belittling his fallen opponents. It is no surprise that the original Nature Boy was the first wrestler to hold both the WWE Championship and the NWA World Championship. The perennial main-eventer strutted his way to an incredible legacy that still resonates with heel stars to this very day.

Shane Douglas: With his in-ring prowess, ability to cut promos better than just about everyone else, and his natural-born talent, the Franchise should have been a bigger star than he was. Even so, the grappler makes the cut here for his career – most notably his groundbreaking work in Extreme Championship Wrestling. Who could forget his feuds with Taz or Terry Funk? Not many. A character like Douglas is so needed in today's wrestling climate just to mix things up a little.

Ivan Koloff: The bearhug extraordinaire could have called it a career in 1971 when he surprisingly ended Bruno Sammartino's seven-year title reign as WWE Champion. That win was the most surprising thing to happen in wrestling – that is until 'Hacksaw' Jim Duggan and the Iron Sheik were busted driving high together. Anyway, a ruthless Russian Bear, Koloff was an intense and memorable wrestler who sort of looked like Street Fighter's Zangief come to life.

George Steele: Be honest, when you grew up you wanted to do one and one thing only. You wanted to become a professional wrestler not for the fame, glory and accolades of being the next great champion. No, in fact you wanted more than all that. You my friend wanted to chew up turnbuckles and run around hairy-backed and all in front of thousands of fans each and every week. Admit it, you always picked the green ice pop just to mimic your favourite crazy animal of the squared circle. By day he was a mild-mannered professor and by night George Steele was an over the top wrestling original. As unpredictable as can be the Animal, who barely uttered anything worth understanding, was a wild man in the ring, earning himself a Hall of Fame nod and he still remains one of the most talked about wrestling characters of all time. While his days eating turnbuckles seem to be in the rear view, Steele once dabbled in acting playing Tor Johnson in Tim Burton's *Ed Wood* along with Johnny Depp and just recently he penned a book about his tales in the ring.

Vince McMahon: Love him or hate him, Vince McMahon is a genius. He forever changed the wrestling landscape from closed circuit television to pay-per-views to buying out all the competitors in the early 2000s. As a personality off screen he is a shrewd businessman, and on screen his Mr McMahon character is always an entertaining, exaggerated version of himself. From his days of lame commentary to his eventual big reveal as the 'Higher Power' McMahon is not only the top wrestling executive to ever live but a top heel in the industry whose mere intro music ('No Chance!') can generate heat like no other.

McMahon is a forward-thinking, game-changing, ratings-grabbing, SOB who was made for this business and made the business what it is today. No need to call AARP, the chairman of the board will be keeping busy breaking new ground rather than playing in a mah-jong card game at a local Stamford senior centre. Long live the real king of wrestling, Vincent Kennedy McMahon. Before we leave you on that note, we should channel our inner heel and say, 'Come on Vince, cut down the costs of the PPVs. They are killing our wallets!'

17
Heels By Numbers

WE never said the good guys had it easy. Here is a quick look at the baddest of the bad by numbers because as they say it's as easy as 1-2-3…

0: Number of on-air appearances by Eric Bischoff at a WrestleMania event.

1: Rank in which Iran and/or Russia would place in regards to the Iron Sheik's favourite countries during his in-ring promos in which he would work the crowd into a frenzy by continuously degrading the red, white and blue.

1: Number of appearances made by the Flying Nuns, Sister Angelica and Mother Smucker which occurred during the debut of WWE's controversial *Shotgun Saturday Night* television show in the winter of 1997.

2: Number of years in which Tatanka was undefeated before Finland's own Ludvig Borga ended the Native American's run, and adding insult to injury the foreign powerhouse pinned him with just one finger.

2: Surprisingly the number of WWE Tag Team Championships held by Danny and Doug Basham, whose greatest claims to fame were as JBL's Secretaries of Defence. In case you're keeping track at home that's more WWE tag title hardware than the Killer Bees, the Fabulous Rougeau Brothers and the Rockers combined.

3: Mid-card faces beware because when Eric Bischoff decided it was time to abuse his general manager powers he gave a three-minute warning in the form of Rosie and Jamal to cure his boredom during *Raw* segments which he deemed dull and unwatchable.

3:16: At the 1996 King of the Ring tournament Steve Austin changed the face of wrestling forever when he put this exclamation point on his victory speech, 'Talk about your psalms, talk about John 3:16, Austin 3:16 says I just whooped your ass.'

4: WrestleMania 2000 saw a fatal four-way elimination match for the WWE Championship. Does it matter who the four participants were? No. The only thing you need to know is that there was a McMahon in every corner.

4: The most controversial championship in the history of wrestling was conceived by the 'Million Dollar Man' Ted DiBiase when he was unable to buy or capture the WWE Championship. Only four superstars have held the title – the already mentioned DiBiase, Virgil, the Ringmaster and Ted DiBiase Jr.

5: It took all five members of the Spirit Squad to capture the WWE tag titles from Big Show and Kane. The quintet of young grapplers were the thorn in DX's side for a while until the crotch-chopping, glowstick-hoarding duo sent everyone's most hated male cheerleaders packing for good.

6: Number of months it took after his debut for the 'Next Big Thing' Brock Lesnar to capture the King of the Ring title and WWE Championship.

6: The name that Sean Waltman used when he joined the New World Order. The former 1-2-3 Kid in WWE became the sixth member of the supergroup, joining Hogan, Hall, Nash, DiBiase and The Giant (Paul Wight) and becoming Syxx.

6.99: Retail price as listed on wweshop.com for a Fandango 'Daa-Da' foam finger.

12: Record number of appearances by any one wrestler in a Hell in a Cell match over the years by the Undertaker. The Deadman is tied with HHH with six for the most victories since the match's conception at WWE's Badd Blood PPV in 1997.

45: The weight in pounds of perennial midget star Little Tokyo.

45: In seconds the length of Andre the Giant's first and only tainted WWE Championship reign after he sold the belt to Ted DiBiase following the Evil Hebner screwjob on Hulk Hogan's four-year title run.

59:26: Length in time that Ric Flair was a participant in the 1992 Royal Rumble, which he won to be crowned WWE Champion.

60: Number of wrestlers who competed in WCW's World War 3 pay-per-view which is by many considered to be a heel turn from the traditional 20-man over-the-top battle royal. It is a three-ring circus – literally.

173: Goldberg's wins before Scott Hall and a cattle prod ended his undefeated streak, enabling Kevin Nash to capture the WCW title in controversial fashion.

434: Number in days of CM Punk's WWE Championship title reign, the longest in the modern era.

822: The combined weight in pounds of King Kong Bundy and Big John Studd, who were Bobby Heenan's answer to the Giant Machine.

06830: Zip code of the Mean Street Posse – Pete Gas, Joey Abs and Rodney – who ruled the streets of their affluent neighbourhood of Greenwich, Ct. before bringing their intimidating sweater vests and supposed toughness to the WWE.

18
Heel Wrestlers A-Z – Last Will And Testament

WELCOME to Heel High School – our graduating seniors will likely go on to bigger and better things but for now, we leave them with this…

A is for Abyss, as in we leave to Abyss Kane's unmasked gimmick so he can steal that concept, too.

B is for Buff Bagwell, who we leave a new WWE contract to replace the one he blew in 2001.

C is for Steve Corino, who we leave some new bleach blond hair dye to replace his existing bleach blond hair dye.

D is for Jim Duggan, who we leave a box of matches and gasoline to burn his Team Canada jacket.

E is for Bob Ellis, who we leave a better-fitted cowboy hat.

F is for Fit Finlay who we leave a Hornswoggle in a box for Christmas.

G is for 'Superstar' Billy Graham, who we leave a videotaped copy of his 'meatball parm' looking like surgery from his second run in WWE.

H is for Haku, who could use a better hairdresser. Perhaps Zohan.

I is for Prince Iaukea, who we leave a paper and a pen to write us an apology for the Artist Formerly Known as Prince Iaukea gimmick.

J is for Jeff Jarrett, who we leave a brand new guitar to hit himself over the head with any time he utters the word 'slappy'.

K is for Kanyon, because few were better than Kanyon.

L is for Joanie Laurer as in Chyna as in keep your clothes on. We leave her a bag of clothes.

M is for Mr Anderson, AKA Mr Kennedy, who we leave a big bag of potential because he clearly lost it.

N is for the nWo, who we leave a comeback on WWE TV but only if Hall, Nash, and Hogan are involved and X-Pac stays home.

O is for Randy Orton, who we leave a new, Viper-free gimmick that expands on his already storied career.

P is for Page, as in Diamond Dallas Page, who we leave a thank-you note for bringing Jake 'The Snake' Roberts and Scott Hall back to life.

Q is for quiche because no wrestler has a last name that starts with Q.

R is for Dusty Rhodes, who we leave Goldust face paint to create the best father–son tandem in wrestling history.

S is for Sting, who we leave an original gimmick – something he has never had in his career.

T is for Tazz, who we leave a new run in the ring and a vacation from the announce booth. A step ladder, too.

U is for the Ultimate Warrior, who we leave a *Promos for Dummies* book.

V is for Volkoff, as in Nikolai Volkoff, who we leave studio time to record his follow-up to 'Cara Mia'.

W is for Whipwreck, Mikey Whipwreck, whose namedrop in this book is enough of a plug.

X is for Xena because nothing starts with X.

Y is for Yokozuna, who we leave a mix tape because his theme song soothed us while we got a back rub and a rub and tug.

Z is for Zeus, who we leave a brand new push to take on Hulk Hogan in Impact Wrestling. No one watched it then, no one will watch it now.

Afterword

FANS make wrestling what it is today, and what it's always been, brudda. I still get such a rush going into the squared circle, and hearing them cheer for me. I even get excited to see how passionate they are shouting at the bad guys. There have been so many great bad guys in wrestling. There have been plenty of awesome heels throughout history from Don Muraco to Ray Stevens. I loved them all – I loved working against them. They were and are my brothers.

I also loved working as a heel. I used to go back and forth in the territories. That's how it was back then. You'd wrestle for a bit as a good guy, and then when things got stale or you wanted to shake things up, you'd turn bad. There are things to like about both – being good and being a bad guy. Being a bad guy, though, was more fun!

Back in the day, I used to love locking up with Ricky Steamboat. He and I told great stories together, and I used to eat it up when the fans would get on my back.

Afterword

I loved getting the heat from the fans – they cared so deeply about everything.

You've got to understand that back then, it was a different time. Fans believed what they saw in the ring. If they saw you against a good guy at an event, they thought you were enemies out of the ring. I loved Captain Lou Albano, and he was a real nemesis for me in the storylines. One day, we were at a beach in Atlantic City hanging out, and a fan thought he was trying to come at me and we had to get the hell out of there, brudda. That's just how it was.

When I came to the World Wrestling Federation, I started out as a heel but it didn't last long. They tried me out as a bad guy at first, but it didn't take. The fans wanted to love the Superfly because of all the things I could do in the ring and on the top rope. I love the fans, and the fans loved me. Like I said, the fans make this business what it is. As long as the fans keep watching, there will always be pro wrestling. It's timeless – just like the heels you read about in this book!

Jimmy 'Superfly' Snuka

About The Authors

JON Chattman experienced his first heel turn when his father took him to see a wrestling card at Nassau Coliseum but left to avoid delays in the parking lot before the main event. While he was eternally grateful to his dad for taking him to the show (and buying him a Hogan foam finger), he really wanted to see Hulk Hogan take on One Man Gang. Missing out on the match barely touches the surface of heel turns the co-author has experienced from a former friend tossing candy at him after *The Matrix* to the creators of *Lost* pulling the plug on their own show after five seasons.

Heel turns aside, Chattman has had a fruitful career thus far.

Chattman has been a writer and blogger for over 15 years, specialising in film, television and music. His online A-Sides Music series (asidesmusic.com), which debuted in August 2011, has garnered praise for its informal style and has been a 'must' destination for rising musicians and established artists and has appeared on Huffington Post, and *USA Today*'s Pop Candy.

He is the author of several notable pop culture and sports-centric books including *How the Red Sox Explain New England* (Triumph Books, 2013), *Superfly: The Jimmy Snuka Story* (Triumph, 2012), *A Battle Royal in the Sky* (Pitch Publishing, 2012), and *I Love the Red Sox, I Hate the Yankees* (Triumph, 2011). Those books were follow-ups to 2009's *Sweet 'Stache*, a humour book on notable celebrity moustaches, and 2006's *Rock On!*, a collection of rock concert memories.

His writing has also appeared in *The New York Post, Wizard, Ultimate Marvel Magazine,* and *TV Guide* to name a few. Chattman has also run thecheappop.com pop culture humour and interview site since 2005.

In addition to his writing, Chattman has had many photographs published, and promotes live music and comedy events in and around Westchester County, NY, and New York City. He was selected as one of the Rising Stars – Westchester's Forty Under Forty by the Business Council of Westchester in 2011.

Chattman lives in Westchester County with his wife, son, and no dog.

Rich Tarantino is a noted author and wrestling enthusiast. He is the author of *Sweet 'Stache: 50 Bad Ass Mustaches and the Faces That Sport Them*, a book chronicling the best celebrity moustaches of all time as well as *I Love the Red Sox, I Hate the Yankees*, a humorous book highlighting the greatest rivalry in the history of sports. His book *A Battle Royal In The Sky:*

The Life and Death of Wrestling's 100 Greatest Gods and Gimmicks, filled with humorous poignancy, celebrates both 50 legends we lost, and 50 gimmicks that have come and gone.

Tarantino experienced his greatest heel moment when he formed the United Super Powers with WWE Hall of Famer Nikolai Volkoff in the summer of 2008 and proudly stood for the Russian National Anthem in front of family and friends. Tarantino once gave his friend a concussion after a botched knee drop from a lifeguard's chair and he first found out how 'real' wrestling was witnessing a match in Wildwood, New Jersey between Haku and Brutus Beefcake from his third row seat. As far as Santa Claus, well that's a whole other story.

Tarantino lives in New York City with his wife, son and two dogs.

The authors watched the World Wrestling Federation (WWF) as it was, before it became World Wrestling Entertainment following a legal ruling in 2002, but have used the term WWE – which the company is now simply called – throughout this book for ease and the avoidance of any confusion.

Special Thanks

JON Chattman would like to thank his tag-team partner Rich Tarantino for lacing his boots once again and entering the ring with me for a book we're so passionate about. Rich – you are the Rene Dupree to my Sylvain Grenier (or Rob Conway). Thank you to Pitch Publishing for reuniting the *Battle Royal in the Sky* duo on this project. It's always a pleasure working with you and your team to create the best product possible.

Thanks to Tommy Dreamer for the foreword, Jimmy Snuka for the afterword, and the wrestling talent that took time out to send us a heel list or story highlighting their favourite baddies of yesteryear. Speaking of which, thanks to all of the fans who shared their personal favourite heel stories in this book. Without the fans, wrestling means very little.

On the personal side of things, I'd like to thank my friends and family, who provide me with the support I need. My parents Gary and Patti have always been a source of strength. I'm so thankful to have them in my life, in my corner, and as 'Nannie' and 'Grandpa' to my son. Friends like Allie Tarantino, John Miele, and Andrew Plotkin keep me sane, and I thank them for that. It's a hard thing to do. Thanks to my nephew Ryan for painting the town red in Vegas with myself and Cousin Sausage.

Thanks to all of the wrestling heels I grew up watching and idolising. Without guys like 'Macho Man' Randy Savage, Jake 'The Snake' Roberts, and to a lesser degree Iron Mike Sharpe on my TV each Saturday morning and Monday night, none of this would have been possible. I'd like to thank the following for no reason: Phil Orient, Pickwick Village, *Dragons' Den*, the Pesky Pole, Vinnie from the Bronx, Scunz, Steve Sommers here and you there, and that cleaning woman at McDonald's who constantly cleaned the floor while we wrote some of this.

Most of all, I'd like to thank my son Noah for his daily inspiration. You are my everything and I love you so much monkey! Thanks also to my wife Alison for her patience with all of my exploits in the world of journalism, blogging, book writing, and show promoting. I love you to pieces. This book is for Kamala, because someone should dedicate something to Kamala.

Rich Tarantino would like to thank his tag partner and friend Jon Chattman for once again reuniting the greatest tag team since Teckno Team 2000. Moustaches, dead wrestlers, red socks and heel turns – what is next? Thanks to Pitch Publishing for putting

Special Thanks

together another amazing book and letting these two jabronis get another shot in the ring.

Special thanks to the 'Innovator of Violence' Tommy Dreamer for the foreword and to Jimmy 'Superfly' Snuka for the afterword. Thanks to all the fans and wrestlers who also shared some of your personal stories for the book.

Thanks to my parents Ralph and Diane for your continued love and support and yes I promise to explain one day why I have all those wrestling masks in the attic. Thanks to Allie Tarantino for the WrestleMania VHS box set and for his vast knowledge of all things New Breed.

I would now like to thank all those who have helped feed my wrestling obsession over the years. In some way, shape or form this book is for all of you: Bert Daddy Cool, Chip Barone, Senor Miele, Joe and Rachel Amori, Kurt (K-pac) Rudolph, P. Daddy Justice, Straight Albert Yankovich, Rich Kosiba, George Marcin, 'Prime Time' Brian Rosa (The Westenders 4 Life), Nathan (Dr Franken) Smith, Big Joe, Clutch King III, Frank 'Poppa' Rodriguez, Moises Budden, Gary Perkowitz, The Puma, The Kommish, everyone at the Pyramid Palace, Deb Ryan, Freaky Bob, and yes even you Mr Goodbody – because of your heel turn I have the honour of being the prestigious winner of the possibly chipped 2013 Pop Goes the Culture 'Body of Work' award.

I want to thank my wife Erica for her love, support, dealing with me and my Monday night obsessions as well as my weekend date nights at McDonald's with Jon and the free Grimace-less wi-fi. It's amazing how long you can McLinger for just two small cokes. Lastly I would like to thank my superhero Jaxon Tarantino for being daddy's favourite champion. I love you this much and more.

Jon Chattman and Rich Tarantino would like to collectively thank Paul and Jane Camillin of Pitch Publishing for getting back into the ring with us on this project. We enjoyed our time working on *A Battle Royal in the Sky: The Life and Death of Wrestling's 100 Greatest Gods and Gimmicks* in 2012, and this ride was just as much fun.

The authors also wish to thank Tommy Dreamer for his foreword and the following wrestling talents who shared their stories on the squared circle with us: Jimmy 'Superfly' Snuka, Ricky 'The Dragon' Steamboat, Zach Gowen, Ata Johnson, and Justin Credible.

Jon and Rich would also like to single out Allie Tarantino for all the stress-free trips to Boston, and dimly lit rides on the Merritt. In all seriousness, we both love you and take it from us 'parents just don't understand'. We'll see you at The Book Shack for our next signing.

They thank their wives, sons, and families for their ongoing support with their obsession over the days of spandex and the nights of Kuklis.

The tag team would also like to thank every single fan who shared their story on their favourite heels or

Special Thanks

heel moments, notably Andrew Plotkin, Kurt Rudolph, Rachel Amori, Matt Bergin, Sean McCallon, Bill Ritter, Steve Sposili, Nicholas Masci, Nicholas Silverstein, Ryan Will, Jon Langford and so many others.

Kim Chee had nothing to do with this book, but someone should thank him for something...so there you have it. Congratulations on your stellar handling of the Ugandan Giant.

No heel book would be complete without heels to write about. With that obvious statement made, Jon and Rich would especially like to thank all the bad guys who are featured in this book. We grew up worshipping so many of the wrestlers featured in this book, and they kept us watching as we ate our breakfast cereal in the morning, our WWE ice creams in the afternoon, and caught a midnight snack while being tucked in our beds covered with wrestling sheets.

We would also like to thank the following people for all that they do and do so well. Here is the list in no particular order, however, if we did put this in order it would probably play out the same way: John Miele, Jr., Anthony DeCicco, Keith Troy, Max Steiner, Spinderella, Cousin Frankie, Vicki the Robot, Deb Ryan, Mario Scarano, Ronald McDonald and his wi-fi, Rich Kosiba, Gary Perkowitz, Rihanna, The Nook Nook, Barney Ross, Angie Frissore, Greasy Grizwald, Scunz, Gusano Loco for closing so early, Seymour Spoons, and finally the Contra codes that got us through our grade-school years. Now press Up, Down, Up, Down, Left, Right, Left, Right, A,

B, A, B, Select, Start when 'Jungle' appears on your screen.

This book is dedicated to Adam 'MCA' Yauch. He probably wasn't a wrestling fan but he inspired so many of us creative types so we want to offer our love and respect to the end.

Epilogue

Author Heel Turn – A Jerry Maguire-Like Mission Statement Rant From Steve's Friend

I STOPPED watching shortly after Shawn Michaels super-kicked Marty Jannetty into oblivion. It had nothing at all to do with the Heartbreak Kid. It had everything to do with me growing out of it and the product growing a bit stale. As a Hulkamaniac, perhaps I never got over the fact the Ultimate Warrior beat him and I just wanted to escape the brand as soon as I could.

In any event, I went nearly a decade before I got back into watching wrestling on a regular basis. It all played out during senior year of college in 1997 and 1998. My best friend Steve, who I grew up with, had continually told me during the spring semester that wrestling had 'gotten good again'. He, of course, was talking about World Championship Wrestling, which had brought back all the greats from my childhood like 'Macho Man' Randy Savage, the 'Immortal' Hulk Hogan, and Bret Hart.

He would tell me week-to-week as we ignored our college professor during class how Hulk Hogan was a bad guy now, and how there's a pay-per-view each month, and how it was a three-hour show called *Nitro*. This would be the norm for weeks, possibly months. Steve would try to sway me to watch week in and week out, and I'd constantly dismiss him until finally one week I just uttered, 'I'll watch once Jim "The Anvil" Neidhart comes back.'

It was meant to be a joke. I just randomly tossed out a name that came to mind, and figured it was obscure enough that it'd never turn into reality. And then, it did.

One Monday night, I got the call. It was Steve. 'Turn on TNT,' he told me. Now, I had never watched anything on Turner Network Television so I had to channel surf for five minutes before I even landed there. Then, lo and behold there he was in the flesh on TV – in living colour – wicked beard and all: Jim Neidhart. Yep, he was back and almost instantly I fell back in love with wrestling.

I was struck immediately by how good Hulk Hogan, a childhood icon of mine, was at being so damn bad. I marvelled at talents like Eddie Guerrero, Goldberg, and The Giant, who was rumoured to be Andre the Giant's son. Of course, the man who would go on to become Big Show isn't related to that lovable French guy but I dug the back story anyway.

Epilogue

Most of all, I was just happy to watch my favourites like Savage back in the ring with a New World Order twist. From then on, every time Steve and I were together we'd talk about *Nitro* or – to a lesser degree – its sister show *Thunder*. We were kids again even though we were months away from graduating college.

As time went on, we'd start to use wrestling lingo like 'Hey yo' a la Scott Hall and even took some lines from Konnan's in-ring promos. Don't hold the latter against us.

Eventually, Steve and I would get together – his house or mine – and watch *Nitro* together. It beat talking to each other on the phone during it, and besides, during commercial breaks, we'd actually play-wrestle each other. One night, as a matter of fact, I accidentally followed through on a piledriver and gave him a bruise on the top of his head.

Weeks later in the hallway of our college while on a ten-minute break from class, he'd fake Ralph Macchio-kick me only to actually make contact with my index finger, bending it all the way back. When we returned to class, my finger gradually became blue and swollen. The next day, I went to the doctor to find out it was sprained. I told the doctor I jammed it another way. After all, how many 22-year-olds go to the doctor for an injury involving play-fighting in a college hallway?

As time went on, Steve and I bought pay-per-views, went to live events, and incorporated 'too sweet' into our vernacular. We'd give each other the Wolfpack hand gestures every time a hot girl walked past us at a bar or if we did something funny or cool or neither. Steve actually made his AOL screen name SJS2Sweet at one point. Damn, those were good times.

After a few years, however, we both stopped watching. The product got stale again, Vince McMahon purchased WCW in 2001, and our *Nitro* parties for two were retired for good.

The product, in this author's opinion, has been a hard sell ever since. John Cena is a company man. He does a great job at entertaining kids but there's something missing. Now, I realise that it could totally be because I'm not a 12-year-old and perhaps Hulk Hogan was my John Cena when I was growing up, but wrestling needs to look back to its past to ensure a future where not just tweens and virgins living at home with their mum can watch it.

The psychology is gone. The build-up is gone. We live in an age where we want immediate results. We text to avoid long phone calls. We e-mail to avoid confrontations. We Skype because we can't visit. We post photos because we don't want to print photos. We live in an age where everything needs to happen right now.

Wrestling is no different. For the better part of the decade, stars have been big guys first, and talent second. With the exception of CM Punk, how many wrestlers over the past decade haven't had a physique that rivalled Batista's? Few. Bobby Lashley got a huge push because he was a big guy. Tyson Tomko got mileage on TV because, again, he was big and had a dynamic look to him. But the substance wasn't there.

Batista had great mic skills and a body to match, and deserved the push he got. Ditto for Brock Lesnar, and other grapplers who took main events. But, because the writing wasn't there, it never played out as well as it could have.

Wrestling still has its share of amazing talents who are smart in the ring and out. Chris Jericho is a wonderful throwback to a time where the build-up mattered more than the brawn. Santino Marella brings out the kid in all of us and reminds us of 1980s wrestling where not taking yourself so seriously could truly entertain. Kurt Angle did a great job of this back in his co-pilot days working alongside 'Stone Cold' Steve Austin.

Wrestling needs more slapstick. It needs more 'Kumbaya' moments. And on the flip side, it needs some blood, sweat, and tears. Two big guys going at it in the ring isn't enough. Two high-flyers doing their thing isn't enough to entertain the masses. Having a cartoon character who rips off taglines from Muhammed Ali and dresses like a middle school misfit can only take you so far.

It's always the same thing. A wrestler starts a feud with someone so quickly that the match happens within a month of the very first promo. That's not the way you build something up. Paul Orndorff didn't just turn on Hulk Hogan randomly one day. He didn't just break into a Piper's Pit segment out of the blue and challenge him to a match. It played out for weeks, and the two greats worked so well against each other because the viewer at home knew they knew each other so well. That's what's missing.

Substance is missing. I want to see CM Punk speak from the heart like he did in a 'is it a shoot or work' fashion two years ago, but I want to see it go somewhere. I want to see Triple H tear down the fourth wall for real, and have him and Vince McMahon go at it on TV with their mouths first and their muscles second, or third.

Wrestling needs to evolve. WWE needs to. Impact Wrestling needs to get some balls. Storylines have been done before, done again, and spit out time and time and time again. Going back to the roots may not be a bad thing. Why not work a kayfabe throwback angle where you show a good guy hanging out with a bad guy on camera as part of a TMZ-type exposé? For example, on *Raw* you set up a match with Big Show taking on a guy like Dolph Ziggler. Then you show on *SmackDown* footage that had been obtained – or better yet run that shit on Twitter or Facebook in the days between the two shows – showing Ziggler and Show throwing down drinks and having a good time at a local bar.

You could then have the *Raw* general manager now call them out, and expose that it's all part of a master plan Ziggler and Show have. I have no clue where I'm going with this, but the bottom line is the writing needs to get better.

Without a solid storyline, it's totally irrelevant who you have going at it in the ring. The reason Ricky 'The

Dragon' Steamboat and 'Macho Man' Randy Savage had such solid feuds was because there were so many moving parts to the storyline (George 'The Animal' Steele was courting Miss Elizabeth on the side), and the two told a story in the ring.

They didn't just hit each other. They didn't just start a feud one night with one killer promo setting a WrestleMania match into action like, for example, Triple H did against Brock Lesnar in 2013. It's done so often we probably don't even realise it.

We live in an age of online spoilers, leaks, and other nonsense. Hey WWE – why not start spreading fake spoilers so you can actually surprise the audience a little?

This jumbled story is brought to you by a fan who remembers being a kid again watching *Nitro* with his friend Steve. He remembers vividly when Goldberg won the title from Hogan because he was glued to it, watching with Steve and his dad on the night after they watched a pay-per-view together.

This jumbled story is brought to you by a kid who was blown away by the storyline of Andre turning on Hogan, of Piper hitting Snuka with a coconut, and even the Ultimate Warrior rambling on a promo.

What wrestling needs is less talk in the ring, and more action.

What wrestling needs is more talk behind the scenes, and less one-night stands from former greats. What wrestling needs is a leader who can take the ball and run with it without pumping his kicks. Right now, we can't see you. We can't see you for the product you can be.

Wrestling has a history of peaks and valleys, but in this technological, fast-moving, short-attention-span theatre world, you have to give us something or else, you're just wasting our time.

Bobby Lashley didn't last for a reason. Tyson Tomko didn't last for a reason. We need more of The Miz and less of the misses. Do you smell what I'm cookin'? It's called substance and it's been lacking for too damn long. Time for Santino to be the general manager, and time for some new grapplers with enough balls to take a survey and say 'Hey yo'.

Yet Another Heel Turn: Tears For A Clown, An Ode To My Folks And The Spanish Word For Moustache

From the yellow polka dots on Dusty Rhodes's trunks to Lex Luger's Total Package, the world of professional wrestling has been there, done that and then some. In what has been proclaimed by the masses as a male soap opera, wrestling fans have been granted access to quite a few of these more outrageously unforgettable moments. Thankfully I have been able to bear witness to the ever-changing carousel of wrestling outrageousness and like a true wrestling enthusiast (that's crazy talk for fanatic) I'd like to share some of them with you…

Epilogue

In 2013 the wrestling world lost yet another personality way too soon. At 55 years young Matt Osborne collapsed at his home and was later pronounced dead on his way to a local hospital. Osborne was a very well rounded wrestler and for decades he fought in and out of the wrestling territories as 'Maniac' Matt Borne. His first high-profile push was as Big Josh, a jean shorts-wearing woodsman during the early years of World Championship Wrestling. This of course would be Osborne's first foray into the cartoonish land of over the top wrestling gimmicks.

It wasn't until he went back to WWE (he had appeared at WrestleMania I when jobbing to Ricky Steamboat) that he was given the full cartoon gimmick treatment in the form of an evil clown with a green wig, greasepaint and a custom-made spandex clown suit – at a time when the wrestling world resembled a three-ring circus complete with hockey goons, garbage men, and something called Bastian Booger.

Vince McMahon, the mastermind behind most if not all gimmicks that have come through his Stamford doors, must have thought there was no better time than now to unleash his evil clown creation on the world and thus Matt Osborne's life was forever changed when he laced up his first pair of clown shoes (probably just some old pair of wrestling boots) and became Doink the Clown.

The reason I bring up Doink is because unknown to him Osborne's clown gimmick (and let's not fool ourselves, Steve Lombardi and Steve Keirn could not perform the patented 'Whoopee Cushion' finisher quite like the Maniac) has stood the test of time and he belongs among the pantheon of legendary characters that was both compelling (yes a bit creepy) and entertaining and true to a great wrestling performer – he always left you wanting more.

The point I am trying to make and I have been joking about this for years with my fellow wrestling brethren (just a couple of good kids who probably play-wrestled in their parents' backyards and watched pay-per-views on illegal black boxes) is that Osborne was not just a guy in clown tights, he was actually a pretty damn good wrestler who just happened to like playing pranks on others.

In fact he helped define an era of pro wrestling that in essence bridged the gap between two greater forces. During the 1980s wrestling was being spearheaded by larger-than-life characters, in particular a certain red and yellow-clad superstar by the name of Hulk Hogan, perhaps the single most recognised gimmick known to the wrestling man and beyond.

Some years later a guy named 'Stone Cold' Steve Austin showed up in our living room every Monday night and taught us all how to disrespect authority, tell a good story and raise holy hell whenever and wherever possible.

Cue the evil clown music shall we, because what ultimately lies in between these colossal years of wrestling greatness is a certain blend of unmistakably bad (but quite often entertaining) and somewhat satisfying storytelling surrounded by real life cartoon characters (that includes you too, Damien Demento).

In other words the genius of Osborne's work as an evil clown should not be forgotten and for that reason alone I stand firmly behind my statement that the Doink era is just as important as the Hogan era or the Austin era. If anything it filled a hole in our wrestling hearts and bridged a gap between two historically iconic figures that defined their respective eras.

A long-running tradition that goes along with tying the knot is the unofficial end to bachelorhood and the all-inclusive debauchery that goes along with the final night of living the single life. For most it is a last trip down memory lane with your old pals getting wasted and making a complete ass of yourself. It is that last hurrah and a time-honoured rite of passage that usually leads to lots of booze and in most cases a gentlemen's club or three.

For me personally my final path to the altar and my last night as a bachelor included booze and the company of great friends and family (even you Bert) but missing from the bachelor party menu that night was the clamouring of buxom beauties ready to send this happy little soon-to-be-married guy off into matrimonial bliss.

Thanks to a few phone calls and I am sure a few hundred bucks from my buddies I got to spend my last night as a single dude singing karaoke with none other than WWE Hall of Famer Nikolai Volkoff.

Volkoff was part of the 1980s wrestling era and a huge star. He was a tag team champion with the Iron Sheik and he was also a star on the *Rock and Wrestling* Saturday morning cartoon. However, despite playing the bad guy for many years Volkoff was a great guy the entire evening and was sharing stories, taking pictures, signing autographs and singing all night with the boys and I.

It was truly an honour to share my final hours not with a well-endowed brunette but with a very classy yet larger-than-life childhood hero who not only helped pave the way for my love of wrestling over the years but on that night he also offered me some genuine marriage advice that I will never ever forget, 'No matter what, she's always right.' And in case you were wondering, yes, he did sing the Russian National Anthem.

I have always wanted to be a part of the wrestling world ever since I pretended I was sleeping on my parents' couch and caught a glimpse of Jimmy 'Superfly' Snuka launching off of Andre the Giant's massive shoulders on to a beaten and battered Samoan. Did it matter who it was, Afa? Sika? No, all that mattered to me was that I was hooked and that I had found my calling. From that moment on I knew wrestling was going to be riding shotgun in my drive through life.

I had always been drawn to the villains of pro wrestling before this whole grey area, from back when everything was simply just black and white. I was the kid cheering on the Dream Team while everyone else was getting moist for the Bulldogs.

Ironically my favourite of all time was Ricky Steamboat, a guy who through my knowledge never dressed in the heel locker room and never stuffed a foreign object into his dragon trunks.

Like all kids growing up in the 1980s I was also a mark for the leg drop but I don't think even if I was an eight-year-old kid growing up in today's day that I would have been sold on the five-knuckle shuffle ending any and all a heel's night.

I knew at some point that if I were ever given a chance to be in a real ring that my calling would be of the villainous persuasion and thankfully for a friend in high places (well actually he just happens to be very tall for his age) my one and only chance came when I got the call from Senor Miele, a local promoter who like me has a passion for the business (his being a little more obsessive than mine if that's even possible).

He told me he was looking for a scrawny and less physically fit man (the fur chest was a complete coincidence) who could play the role of his bodyguard during a main event match that he was planning for his wrestling swansong (all the great ones get pulled back in John, they always do).

So there I was playing the role of the enforcer for a guy who was putting his hair on the line (classic bad guy move) in a match between two of the best mini-wrestlers ever, Mascarita Dorada and Pierrothito. I felt like the Black Scorpion (that's not a good thing) but I resembled the third Mulkey (that's definitely not a good thing). However, I enjoyed every second under the hood as a true in-ring wrestling rule-breaker billed as El Bigote.

It should be noted that fellow New Rochelle native Devon 'Dudley' Hughes and I have a combined total of 23 World Tag Team Championships between the two of us. Of course you can do the maths, in fact during my in-ring encounter (I think you have to make contact for it to actually be considered an encounter) I did not win any gold but thanks to Senor Miele and others I felt like a true champion and at the very least a legit rule-breaker (at least that's what I can tell the grandkids).

My parents never took away my passion to watch wrestling. In fact they even feed my desire – if you know my dad then I am sure you've heard the Junkyard Dog Buffalo story and my mum once took one for the team and got us lost in New Jersey just so we could catch a glimpse of the spectacle that is pro wrestling (Get the snake out!).

One of these days my son Jaxon will tell me about the time he pretended to be asleep as he watched CM Punk drop an elbow on John Cena (it's a heel book so keep dropping those 'bows on the Cenation) and I clamour for the day that we can sit ringside at an actual wrestling event and cheer on our favourite bad guys.

Welcome to my three-ring circus Jax. Welcome to the greatest show on earth.